Unlocking the Wisdom of I Ching

Alma M. Choi

All rights reserved. Copyright © 2023 Alma M. Choi

COPYRIGHT © 2023 Alma M. Choi

All rights reserved.

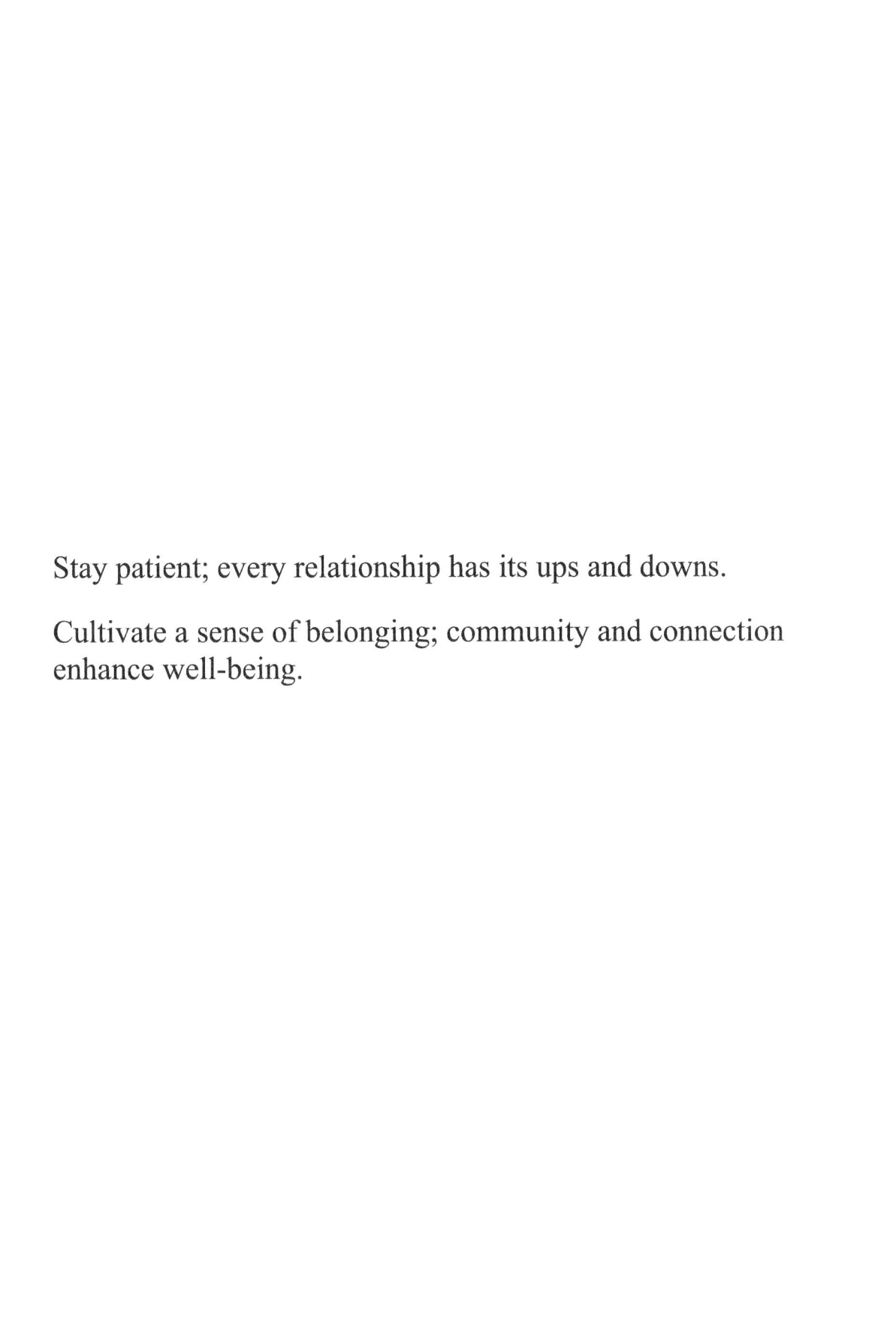

Stay patient; every relationship has its ups and downs.

Cultivate a sense of belonging; community and connection enhance well-being.

Engage in regular brain exercises; activities like reading or puzzles enhance cognitive function.

Engage with books that explore spirituality; they offer insights into the deeper aspects of existence.

Introduction

Step into the profound world of divination and wisdom with this bool. This guide serves as a gateway to unlocking the timeless insights of the I Ching, an ancient Chinese oracle that has captivated hearts and minds for centuries. Delve into the rich history, philosophical underpinnings, and practical applications of this remarkable system as you embark on a journey of self-discovery and enlightenment.

Unveiling the Historical Tapestry: Begin your exploration by unwrapping the layers of history that shroud the I Ching. Discover the origins of this revered oracle and its significance across various historical epochs. From ancient Chinese dynasties to its influence on East Asian countries and even its impact on European philosophies, the I Ching's reach extends far beyond geographical and cultural boundaries.

The I Ching in Modern Times: Delve into the contemporary relevance of the I Ching and its enduring presence in our lives. Explore how its teachings continue to resonate with seekers of wisdom, guiding them through the complexities of modern existence.

Bridging Divination and Practicality: The magic of the I Ching lies in its ability to bridge the mystical with the practical. Learn how to apply its ancient wisdom to your everyday life, using its insights to navigate decisions, relationships, and challenges. Discover how the I Ching can be a trusted companion, providing clarity and perspective when you need it most.

Navigating the Hexagrams: Embark on a comprehensive journey into the intricacies of the I Ching's hexagrams. Uncover the method behind the oracle's divination process and learn to decipher the messages embedded within its intricate patterns. Gain a deeper understanding of the hexagram index and explore the significance of each component in the interpretation.

The Mosaic of Wisdom: Immerse yourself in the heart of the I Ching—the 64 hexagrams that form its core. Each hexagram holds a unique blend of wisdom, offering guidance on everything from personal growth to decision-making. Dive into the narratives of these hexagrams and unravel the threads of insight they weave.

The Path to Divination Mastery: As you tread the path of the I Ching, you'll discover its potential to guide your decisions, illuminate your journey, and foster self-awareness. Immerse yourself in its profound teachings, drawing from its rich history and timeless wisdom to navigate the complexities of existence.

Elevate Your Journey with the I Ching: This book beckons you to embark on an enriching journey of introspection and discovery. As you venture through the pages of this guide, you'll uncover the hidden gems of an oracle that has stood the test of time. Whether you're seeking answers, insights, or a deeper connection to the mysteries of the universe, the I Ching is your compass. Let its teachings empower you to embrace the present, navigate the future, and embark on a journey of wisdom that spans generations.

Contents

The History of the *I Ching* 1
  The Origin of the I Ching 2
in Past and Present Societies 4
    I Ching Hexagram Index 12
    1.   Ch'ien - The Creative 15
    2.   K'un - The Receptive 18
    3.   Chun - Difficulty at The Beginning 20
    4.   Mêng - Youthful Folly 22
    5.   Hsu - Waiting (Nourishment) 24
    6.   Sung - Conflict 26
    7.   Shih - The Army 28
    8.   Pi - Holding Together (Union) 31
    9.   Hsiao Ch'u - The Taming Power Of The Small 33
    10. Lu - Treading (Conduct) 35
    11. T'ai - Peace 37
    12. P'i - Stagnation 39
    13. T'ung Jên - Fellowship With Men 41
    14. Ta Yu - Possession in Great Measure 43
    15. Ch'ien - Modesty 45
    16. Yu - Enthusiasm 47
    17. Sui - Following 49
    18. Ku - Work On What Has Been Spoiled (Decay) 51
    19. Lin - Approach 54
    20. Kuan - Contemplation (View) 56

21.	Shih Ho - Biting Through	58
22.	Pi - Grace	60
23.	Po - Splitting Apart	62
24.	Fu - Return (The Turning Point)	64
25.	Wu Wang - Innocence (the Unexpected)	66
26.	Ta Ch'u - The Taming Power of the Great	68
27.	I - The Corners of the Mouth (ProvidingNourishment)	70
28.	Ta Kuo - Preponderance of the Great	72
29.	K'an - the Abysmal (Water)	74
30.	Li - The Clinging, Fire	76
31.	Hsien - Influence (Wooing)	78
32.	Hêng - Duration	80
33.	Tun - Retreat	82
34.	Ta Chuang - the Power of the Great	84
35.	Chin - Progress	86
36.	Ming I - Darkening of the Light	88
37.	Chia Jên - the Family (Clan)	90
38.	K'uei - Opposition	92
39.	Chien - Obstruction	94
40.	Hsieh - Deliverance	96
41.	Sun - Decrease	98
42.	I - Increase	100
43.	Kuai - Breakthrough (Resoluteness)	102
44.	Kou - Coming to Meet	104
45.	Ts'ui - Gathering Together (Massing)	106
46.	Shêng - Pushing Upward	108
47.	K'un - Oppression (Exhaustion)	110

48. Ching - the Well 112
49. Ko - Revolution (Molting) 114
50. Ting - the Caldron 116
51. Chen - the Arousing (Shock, Thunder) 118
52. Kên - Keeping Still, Mountain 120
53. Chien - Development (Gradual Progress) 122
54. Kuei Mei - the Marrying Maiden 124
55. Fêng - Abundance (Fullness) 127
56. Lu - the Wanderer 129
57. Sun - the Gentle (the Penetrating, Wind) 131
58. Tui - the Joyous, Lake 133
59. Huan - Dispersion (Dissolution) 135
60. Chieh - Limitation 137
61. Chung Fu - Inner Truth 139
62. Hsiao Kuo - Preponderance of the Small 141
63. Chi Chi - After Completion 143
64. Wei Chi - Before Completion 145

The Book of Divination and Wisdom 147

The History of the *I Ching*

As the *I Ching* is an ancient divination text, it has a lot of history. Understanding where the first divination text came from and how it came to be is an important part of connecting with the *I Ching* on a personal level.

This section of the book will briefly teach you all about what the *I Ching* was and is-its origins and role in ancient history. Read on for a brief introduction to the *I Ching* or *Book of Changes* and let it bring change to your life, too.

The Origin of the I Ching

According to historians, scholars, and philosophers, the *I Ching* divination text originated over 5,000 years ago. It played a huge role in one of the Chinese dynasties-the Zhou Dynasty.

While today we know the divination text as the *I Ching* (originally read as *Yi Jing)* or the *Book of Changes*, it was originally called *Zhou Yi* (周易), meaning the *Changes of Zhou* during the Western Zhou Dynasty. This simple yet wise divination text has become a classic that many still refer to. Because of its unending wisdom and guidance, many people find that the *I Ching* is the most reliable adviser and friend in times of both trouble and happiness.

While today most people use three coins to perform consultations with the *I Ching*, historically, Chinese divination masters would throw a bundle of fifty yarrow sticks.

This cleromancy-style divination technique was discovered by a great hero of the Zhou dynasty, Fu Xi. By using the yin and yang, the *I Ching* is able to foresee future events and share wisdom based on these two energies that keep the world in balance. In line with this, the *I Ching* does not deny that there is evil in the world-and it does not try to eradicate it. Unlike other divination techniques, the *I Ching* will not tell those who consult it what to do or how to live their lives. Rather, it gives advice somewhat akin to a gentle nudge in the right direction. It is ultimately up to the person to make the decision.

The bundle of yarrow sticks was tossed and interpreted into six lines(爻 yáo), which together were called a hexagram (挂 guà). Depending on how the yarrow sticks fell, the line could be either broken or unbroken. When six lines were formed and the hexagram was completed, the divination master would use the *Zhou Yi* to look up the name of the hexagram (挂名). Each hexagram corresponded to a statement, as did each line. The reading was complete when all the statements had been read-including the changing lines. More about how the *I Ching* is performed and consulted will be discussed in the following chapters.

In history, the *I Ching* advised emperors, farmers, scholars, traders, philosophers, and all kinds of people from different walks of life. People could turn to the *I Ching* and find comfort in knowing that they were never truly alone.

Now that you know when and how the *I Ching* was first used to advise people, read on to learn more about how it has evolved through the ages-and how people have evolved with it.

The Role of the *I Ching* in Past and Present Societies

As was previously stated, the *I Ching* played a major role in historical Chinese dynasties. It also had influence in other parts of East Asia-and even in Europe. Scholars in different parts of the world regarded the *I Ching* as a book that embodied wisdom. While some were skeptical about its divination abilities, few denied that it was a book that brought about progress and change. It forced people to look into themselves and change accordingly.

Ancient Chinese Dynasties

Apart from being an influencer in the Western Zhou Dynasty, the *I Ching* also advised citizens and leaders of the Eastern Han and Tang Dynasties. The Han Dynasty was the golden period of Chinese history, and many believed that the *I Ching* had a hand in its rapid and admirable development.

During the Han Dynasty, the *Zhou Yi* texts gave rise to two contradictory schools of thought-the School of Images and Numbers and the School of Meanings and Principles. These two schools were headed by factions known as the New Text Criticism and the Old Text Criticism, respectively. These separate schools focused on different aspects of the book-logic and morality. They dissected each topic and made their own copies of the *I Ching*. Though most of their texts were lost, some were preserved through efforts of Tang Dynasty scholars.

With the fall of the Han Dynasty, their various writings and teachings became disorganized. While Han scholars were able to create many similar-yet-different systems of divination through studying the *I Ching*, many of these became mixed and confused with other teachings.

Thus, an emperor of the Tang Dynasty commissioned his scholars to create a complete version of the text-the version that we know today-integrating the teachings of both the New and Old Text Criticism teachings.

This consolidated text became a major influencer for many Confucian and Neo-Confucian scholars (e.g. Cheng Yi and Xiao Yong). They were able to use the *I Ching* as a moral compass and integrate its moral teachings into their own schools of thought. Quite by accident, Xiao Yong also developed a binary number system from studying the divination text.

The *I Ching* definitely influenced the dynasties that came before, after, and in between those mentioned above-but the surviving teachings and records of the *I Ching* date back to those two. It can be said that the *I Ching* influenced society as its practices were, in turn, influenced by society.

East Asian Countries

The *I Ching* was not just used in China but also in both Japan and Korea. A Korean neo-Confucian scholar named Yi Hwang wrote a critique on the *I Ching* that had a major influence in both these countries. Ultimately, the *I Ching* teachings and Yi Hwang's critique became influencers in the Silhak reform movement of Korea.

In Japan, on the other hand, two scholars-Kokan Shiren and Yoshida Kanemoto-studied the *I Ching*, critiqued it, translated it, and then copied it out for the multitudes to read. It thus became comparatively more influential in Japanese society than in Korea. The *I Ching* found its way into teachings of numerology, Newtonian mechanics, divination, and Copernican principles, among others.

In both countries, the *I Ching* had a hand in shaping Confucian principles as well as many schools of thought and reform movements.

European Philosophies

The Chinese writing system and culture gained traction in Europe because of the *I Ching*. Two philosophers, Leibniz and Hegel, argued about the legitimacy of the *I Ching* bringing the concept of non-Western ideals into Western society. Leibniz married the binary numbers found in the *I Ching* divination manual to the concept of the Christian God, stating that a broken line cannot change into a whole one without the intervention of the divine.

Hegel, on the other hand, argued that because the Chinese language was made up of symbols and abstraction it could not express valid philosophical ideals. (This claim, though, ignored the historical significance of each Chinese character.)

The I Ching Today

While the *I Ching* played a part in Chinese history and the formation of specific schools of thought, it is no longer an obvious part of mainstream Chinese culture. If one looks deeper into Confucianism teachings, though, he or she will definitely find many *I Ching* philosophies hidden within them. Confucius saw the *I Ching* as a philosophical book rather than as a divination manual, and thus used its teachings and proverbs in his own school of thought. His followers have been doing the same for ages.

Today, the *I Ching* divination manual has been translated into various Western languages over a dozen times. Its teachings are still relevant, and many still rely on its guidance. The *I Ching* has become a way of life for many people. Read on if you want to learn how to integrate the *I Ching* into your life, as well.

Applying the *I Ching* to Everyday Life

Many people see the *I Ching* merely as a divination manual. What they fail to fathom is that consulting the *I Ching* is a way of life-it is not a one-off deal. Seeking guidance from the *I Ching* means *continuously* asking for help and advice-and listening to that advice.

As many philosophers have noticed, the *I Ching* is more than just a book. Its followers are not directly told what the future holds; rather, *I Ching* practitioners are taught how to deal with unforeseen future events, how to live life at peace with others, and how to constantly become better. Thus, consulting the *I Ching* once will never be enough. For true change to come about, the *I Ching* must become a part of everyday life.

This section of the book will teach you everything you need to know to get started on your enlightened journey with the *I Ching*. It will tell you about the basics of the *I Ching*-from casting to the readings-and how it can be used as a guiding force for both everyday and major decisions.

Read on to learn more about the *I Ching* and how it can help your life take a turn for the better.

Getting Started with the *I Ching*

It cannot be stressed enough that consulting the *I Ching* is a way of life. The *I Ching's* guidance must be sought not only during turbulent times, but also for everyday life. Understanding this is very important, because the more one integrates the *I Ching* into his or her daily life, the more accurate the readings get. In turn, if an *I Ching* practitioner follows its teachings and stays true to its practice, enlightenment will follow.

In ancient China, *I Ching* divination practitioners would throw yarrow sticks and glean the readings from their formation upon falling. By interpreting the readings into a hexagram, the consultant was able to gain results. Today, we do things a little differently.

In this generation, the *I Ching* is consulted by tossing three coins. Depending on the combination of heads and tails, a hexagram can be formed.

The first step to consulting the *I Ching* is contemplating your question. This step is optional-if you do not have a question in mind, the *I Ching* will merely evaluate your current state and advise you based on that. If you do have a question, take a few minutes to contemplate it and really get a grip on it in your mind.

The second step is tossing the coins six times. If you have a question, hold it in your mind while doing this. Record the results of each toss. Each face of the coins has a specific value: **heads** has a value of 3, while **tails** has a value of 2. After each toss, compute the total value by adding the values of each coin. Each value corresponds to a line that will make up part of your hexagram.

Each of your tosses will result in one of the following:

Heads	Tails	Total	Yin or Yang	Line Appearance
0	3	6	Yin (changing)	— — — — — ·
1	2	7	Yang	————————
2	1	8	Yin	— — — — — ·
3	0	9	Yang (changing)	————————

The yin and yang are integral parts of each *I Ching* reading. An even total corresponds to yin energy, and an odd total corresponds to yang energy. Yin is represented by a broken line while Yang is represented by an unbroken line. If your toss results in three coins with the same face, it means you have gotten a **changing line** and you will ultimately have two hexagrams.

The third step is to review your results and build your hexagram. A hexagram is built from the bottom up, so your first toss will be the base of the hexagram, or the bottommost line. Remember, the order of your hexagram matters.

Below is an example of a hexagram:

SIXTH LINE	————————	7
FIFTH LINE	— — — — —	6
FOURTH LINE	————————	9
THIRD LINE	— — — — —	8
SECOND LINE	————————	7
FIRST LINE	— — — — —	6

The fourth step is to analyze the two trigrams of your hexagram. Divide your hexagram into two-lines 1, 2, 3 and lines 4, 5, 6. The bottom three lines make up the lower trigram and top three lines make up the upper trigram. Consult the *I Ching* Hexagram Index to find the name of your hexagram. Look for the upper trigram on the horizontal axis and the lower trigram on the vertical axis. The intersection of the two trigrams is the name of your hexagram.

The fifth step is to finally analyze your reading. The reading is made up of three parts: the title and representation, the analysis, and the line-by-line reading. The title and representation will tell you what the hexagram stands for. The analysis will explain the meaning of that hexagram. The line-by-line reading will tell you what is in store for you, or comment on your current state.

After you have identified your hexagram, read the title and representation, and the analysis. After this, identify which lines are changing (i.e. the lines for which you tossed three coins with the same face; the lines with a total value of either 6 or 9) and which lines are unchanging. **Read only the line-by-line reading for the changing lines, for those are the only ones that apply to you directly**. If you arrived at a line by tossing a 7 or 8, it is an unchanging line which is significant only as part of the hexagram; it is meaningless on its own, so the line-by-line reading does not apply.

If you got any changing lines, there's a sixth step of identifying your second hexagram by transforming the changing lines into their opposites (i.e. yin becomes yang, an unbroken line becomes a broken line). Identify your new hexagram once again using the *I Ching* Hexagram Index and read the hexagram's title and representation and analysis.

This second reading will complement your first one. Using the two readings together will help you find the answers you seek.

Even though you now have your reading, make sure to come back and consult the *I Ching* regularly in case there are new developments in your spiritual state. Remember, the *I Ching's* advice is here to help you live your life better and help you find fulfillment.

Whenever you need a little encouragement or a little push in the right direction, consult the *I Ching*. Its sage advice will help you with whatever is troubling you-whether you know it or not.

I Ching Hexagram Index

Upper ▶ / Lower ▼	CH'IEN ☰ Heaven	CHÊN ☳ Thunder	K'AN ☵ Water	KÊN ☶ Mountain	K'UN ☷ Earth	SUN ☴ Wind	LI ☲ Fire	TUI ☱ Lake
CH'IEN ☰ Heaven	1	34	5	26	11	9	14	43
CHÊN ☳ Thunder	25	51	3	27	24	42	21	17
K'AN ☵ Water	6	40	29	4	7	59	64	47
KÊN ☶ Mountain	33	62	39	52	15	53	56	31
K'UN ☷ Earth	12	16	8	23	2	20	35	45
SUN ☴ Wind	44	32	48	18	46	57	50	28
LI ☲ Fire	13	55	63	22	36	37	30	49
TUI ☱ Lake	10	54	60	41	19	61	38	58

Parts of the Hexagram Interpretation

As stated earlier, there are three main parts of a hexagram reading- the title and representation, the analysis, and the line-by-line reading.

Each hexagram has a title (e.g. 乾 is Ch'ien or the Creative). The title gives you a peek at what you must become to overcome a problem or live a better life. The representation has two parts: (1) the judgment; and (2) the image. As Mandarin is a very visual language, there is an image portion to the reading. This will help you imagine what it will be like to fulfill the prophecy.

The judgment is what you must become to fulfill the prophecy. Remember though, the *I Ching* does not predict the future; rather, it tells you how you should act in your current situation. The image is the visual representation of the title (e.g. the Creative can be visualized as "the movement of heaven is full of power," which can be construed as the creativity of clouds).

The next part of the reading is the analysis. Admittedly, the title and representation are quite hard to understand, as they were translated from Mandarin. The analysis part of the reading is an in-depth explanation of the *I Ching's* comments on your current state or its instructions regarding what you must do. It also tells you how you must act towards the *Higher Power* (also referred to as the *Sage*, and by other names).

The last part of the consultation is the line-by-line reading. Again, because Mandarin is a very visual language, it is sometimes hard to understand this portion of the consultation. Do not worry; in this book, we have tried to make sure that everything is clearly explained. Each line corresponds to one of your tosses. Line 1 is your first throw, or the bottommost line on your hexagram, while Line 6 is the topmost. Some lines will have visual representations, while others do not. The number at the beginning of each line reading is your possible toss (i.e. 6 can also be 8, and 9 can also be 7).

Remember, the *I Ching* does not predict the future, nor does it claim to know what will happen next. Rather, it makes sure that you handle each situation you enter with grace and preparedness. Its prophecies merely nudge you in the right direction, guiding you to where you need to be. Though it will sometimes make certain claims about how you must act in response to future events, it will not tell you what those events are.

The next chapter contains readings for all 64 hexagrams of the *I Ching*. Admittedly, it can be quite confusing at times. Sometimes you will not understand what the reading truly means until certain events come to pass. Despite that, we urge you to trust the *I Ching* and make consulting it a daily habit so that the readings will become easier to understand. Start tossing your coins, casting your readings, and walking down the road to a better life.

The 64 Hexagrams of the *I Ching*

1. Ch'ien - The Creative

≡ HEAVEN
≡ HEAVEN

The representation

Judgment
The Creative stands for success and perseverance. If you cast a Ch'ien hexagram, it means that you need to persevere to gain success.

Image
Imagine the heavens. The heavens represent power and strength, hope and peace. The Creative is strong-willed and untiring-s/he overcomes challenges and stays strong through adversity.

Analysis

During this time, you have direct access to the powers of the Creative-a *Higher Power* that you must place your trust in. You must stand firm in your beliefs and principles, never backing down, even in the face of temptation or despair. Tuning yourself to the Creative nature means being kind to others and turning away from your bad habits and ill wishes. It also means having more kindness and understanding towards others and yourself. When you start to lose hope, or feel that things are impossible-remember that everything is not always as it seems and that, with creativity, you can see your situation from a different angle.

Be patient with life, and trust that everything will correct itself when the time is right. Do not strain yourself too hard because you will only hurt yourself. In the same way, do not push others to do things that they cannot or do not want to do, even if the ends are justified.

Above all, be receptive to the *Higher Power* and listen to the Creative power as it guides you to where you need to be. Do not hesitate to call for help when you need it.

Line-by-line reading

Line 1
The first line is a *hidden dragon*. It means that you must not act yet. You must be patient and wait for the Creative to give you a clear go signal.

Line 2
The second line is a *dragon emerging into the field*. It means that you must remain patient and humble. While recognition and achievement may be tempting, do not let your ego guide you.

Line 3
The third line is a *creative superior man*. It means that you know what you need to do, and how to do it-you need only act. But be warned that both ambition and ego can get in the way of what is right. Stay true to your path and make the right choices based on your beliefs.

Line 4
The fourth line is the image of a *dragon about to leap into the deep*. This line means that you are on the verge of doing something important, but you must not rush into your task. Remember to stay alert to the guidance of the *Higher Power.*

Line 5

The fifth line is a *dragon flying in the heavens*. Greatness and possibility have finally merged, and you are now treading the right path. Stay true to your beliefs and keep listening to the Creative.

Line 6
The last line is *an arrogant dragon overlooking the land.* Arrogance will lead you astray. If you stop listening to the *Higher Power*, you will regret your choices. Stay humble and receptive-do not lose hope. Do not give yourself a reason to despair.

All your tosses resulted in 9s, and this signifies good luck. Remember, stay attuned to the Creative and the *Higher Power* and you will find that you have all the tools you need to finish your tasks.

2. K'un - The Receptive

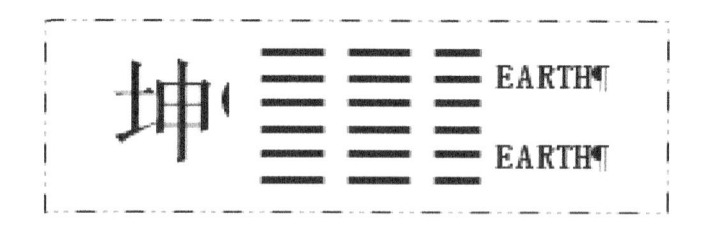

坤 ☷☷ EARTH / EARTH

The representation

Judgment
Like the Creative, the Receptive also stands for perseverance and success. The Receptive, though, emphasizes the importance of staying attuned to the *Higher Power*-following rather than leading.

Image
Imagine the earth as a receptive being. Now, you must be like the earth as it adapts to all its inhabitants.

Analysis

The hexagram you cast means that you must be more attuned to the environment and the people around you. Now is not the time for you to initiate things; rather, it is time to allow yourself to be led to the right path by listening to those around you. Again, you must remain humble and keep your head down while making sure you get the tasks assigned to you done.

As opposed to leading, you must now become the supporter, the follower, and the helper. Stay attuned to the *Higher Power* and allow yourself to become a true follower.

Line-by-line reading

Line 1

The first line is *treading on hoarfrost; solid ground is not too far away.* While things may seem unstable now, keep moving forward and following your leader to where you must go.

Line 2
The second line is *a square arising from straight lines.* Now is not the time to push yourself. Rather, it is time to stay open-minded and let nature take its course. Allow yourself to be guided by the *Higher Power*, and your solution will present itself.

Line 3
The third line is *perseverance when lines are hidden.* This means that you must remain innocent and let go of vanity. Focus on your work without seeking recognition or fame.

Line 4
The fourth line is *a bag that is tied closed.* This is a time to remain inconspicuous, hidden both from external enemies and the temptations of your own ego.

Line 5
Do not draw attention to yourself through your dress or bearing. Let your inner character speak for itself.

Line 6
The last line is *dragons fighting in a field and spilling blood.* Entering into a conflict will only result in injury to both yourself and your opponent, followed by ultimate defeat.

Casting this hexagram, with all 6s, means that you must persevere. With perseverance, everything will fall into place.

3. Chun - Difficulty at The Beginning

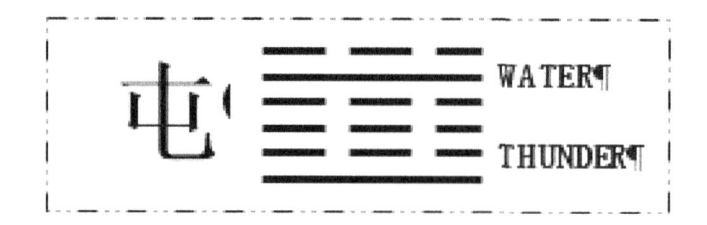

The representation

Judgment
This hexagram means that you will overcome difficulty and come out stronger-but you need to ask for help from those who you can rely on.

Image
Imagine clouds and thunder at the beginning of the storm. After the storm has passed, the superior person can sort things out and achieve his/her goals.

Analysis

The best thing for you to do right now is take it easy and be patient. Now, perseverance means that you must persevere in holding back. After all your hardships, success will finally come. But you must not be hasty, nor must you rely solely on yourself. The *Higher Power* will tell you when it is time to act-but right now, it is time to hold back. It is time to ask for help and to rely on those who can be trusted.

Line-by-line reading

Line 1
Sometimes it is correct to hesitate and hold back temporarily, but keep on persevering. Do not rely solely on yourself-rely on the *Higher Power* to overcome all.

Line 2

The second line is a *retreating chariot*. When you are having a hard time, it does no good to accept help too soon. You must stay patient. If the offer is well-meant, there will be a proper time to accept it.

Line 3
The third line is *one following a deer but finding only himself.* You must rely on the *Higher Power*-let *It* guide you. If you try to do things on your own-either physically or spiritually-you will fail.

Line 4
The fourth line is *a lady in a retreating chariot seeking her partner.* Strive for both unity in the face of difficulties. Do not let your ego or insecurities blind you to opportunities for friendship and cooperation. Two are stronger than one, and the *Higher Power* will reward your strength.

Line 5
The fifth line is *difficulty*. You must not let the doubt of others hinder you from doing what is right. Stand firm in your beliefs and keep believing in the *Higher Power*. Persevere, but do not strain yourself. If you push yourself too hard, you will fail.

Line 6
The last line is a *retreating chariot with its rider crying tears of blood.* Do not stop standing up for your beliefs, no matter what hardships you must endure. While you will be tempted to stray from the path, do not. Perseverance will be rewarded.

4. Mêng - Youthful Folly

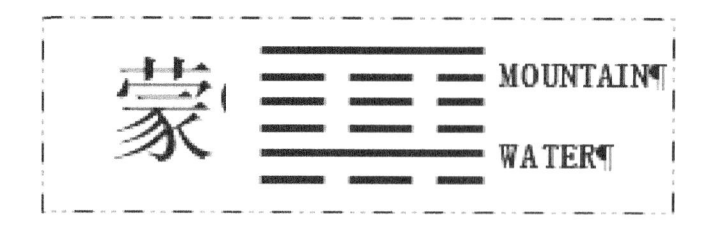

蒙 ☶ MOUNTAIN
☵ WATER

The representation

Judgment
Even those who are foolish can become successful. They need only to follow the *Higher Power* and persevere.

Image
Imagine a spring suddenly appearing at the foot of a mountain. This is the representation of youth-a fresh pool before the steep climb. While you are young, you must start improving yourself.

Analysis

While our ages may differ, we are all young. And the young tend to commit folly. In times of despair, foolhardiness, or doubt, turn to the *Higher Power*, for it will guide you to maturity and wisdom. The *I Ching* is here to guide all of us towards wisdom and a better life. Being young is only the start of your journey. Even if you are foolish now, if you rely on the *I Ching*, you will keep getting wiser.

Line-by-line reading

Line 1
Self-discipline is important for character development. Make sure to keep exercising your character through the *I Ching* and the *Higher Power*, but do not change yourself.

Line 2

As you become wiser, more people will seem foolish to you-treat them kindly and guide them. As you were once foolish, show them the right path.

Line 3
There is no point in blindly following. The *Sage* wants you to seek the truth not because *He* wants you to, but because you want to. Blind allegiance is of no use; use your gift of free will.

Line 4
Learn to identify your foolishness so that you are not humiliated. Do not lose yourself in fears and dreams formed by your ego; rather, stay humble and detached so that you may become wise.

Line 5
The foolishness of a child is not foolishness-it brings good fortune, for it is innocent. To become wise, you must become like a child-open-minded and filled with wonder.

Line 6
Fools must be punished for their actions so that they learn. If you are the fool, learn from your punishments. If you are not, then it is not your place to punish. Leave matters of punishment to the *Higher Power*.

5. Hsu - Waiting (Nourishment)

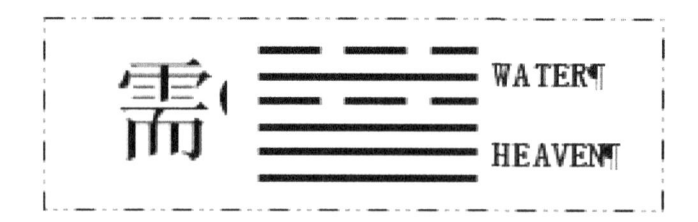

需而 ☵ WATER / ☰ HEAVEN

The representation

Judgment
Sincerity and perseverance are the keys to overcoming challenges and achieving success. Make sure that your motivations are pure.

Image
Imagine how water slowly rises up to the heavens. That is the image of waiting and patience, as water rises up to meet the clouds, right before pouring down.

Analysis

What you need most now is to be patient. They say "good things come to those who wait," so wait you must. While things may seem to be moving at a slow pace, if you remain patient, you open yourself up to the guidance of the *Higher Power*. Keep listening to that guidance, and act *only* when the time is right.

Remember, though, that you need to be gracefully patient. Waiting with impatience will drive away the guidance of the *Higher Power*. You must trust that everything will right itself in due time.

Line-by-line reading

Line 1
The first line is *one waiting in the meadow*. While it may seem like nothing is happening now, be patient and endure so that you will be

ready when something does happen.

Line 2
The second line is *one waiting while standing on sand.* The rough sand signifies adversity, but you must remain still. Keep waiting for things to right themselves, and keep listening to the guidance of the *Higher Power*.

Line 3
The third line is *one waiting while standing in mud*. This signifies that one who will try to sway your ideals will arrive-stand firm. Do not let yourself be wrongly influenced.

Line 4
The fourth line is *one standing in blood*. You are now in grave danger because you refused the help of others and/or the *Higher Power*. Return to your patient waiting state, and accept the help of those who offer it.

Line 5
The fifth line is *one waiting for food and drink*. This means that it is time for a short rest. Take a short break to regenerate so that you can be better prepared to face more challenges.

Line 6
The last line is *one enters a cave and three uninvited guests arrive*. Unexpected events occur, and strange solutions present themselves-but you must welcome them with an open mind.

If you patiently wait, you will have good fortune.

6. Sung - Conflict

訟 ═══════ HEAVEN
── ── WATER

The representation

Judgment
Even when you believe you are in the right, it does not help to push your point so far that you make implacable enemies. Seek compromise, seek impartial mediators, and seek the guidance of the *Higher Power*.

Image
Imagine the waters leaving the heavens-that is the image of conflict. The beginning of conflict is the best time to resolve it; thus, you must carefully consider you path right from the start so that you can easily end it.

Analysis

No matter where it comes from, conflict must be removed. Even if you act with the best of intentions, conflict and opposition will arise. The solution is to take a step back and view the problem through the lenses of integrity, caution, and quiet contemplation.

Conflicts and challenges cause doubt and negative emotions to arise. If you let them overshadow your positive emotions, you will invite more negativity and conflict into your life. Do not encourage conflict. Rather, hold fast to your values, seek guidance from the *Higher Power*, and patiently wait for resolution. Every conflict stems from inner turmoil, so you need to stay at peace with yourself to overcome challenges.

Line-by-line reading

Line 1
The first line is *one ignoring all slander against him*. You must remain apathetic so as not to encourage conflict. People will talk, but if you ignore them, you will meet a fortunate end.

Line 2
The second line is *one who is not ready for conflict.* If you fall into the temptations of your ego, you will fail. If you remain humble and call on the help of the *Higher Power*, you will succeed.

Line 3
The third line *is one who remains in his old place*. If you hold on to your ideals and stay true to yourself, you will not be harmed. You must carry out your duties even when the credit will go to another.

Line 4
The fourth line is *another who is not ready for conflict*. While you may be materially prepared to vanquish an opponent, you must not start a fight for reasons of selfishness and pride. Rather, choose the way of peace and take comfort that you are acting in accord with the *Higher Power*.

Line 5
The fifth line is *one who is equal to the conflict.* When you confront an opponent for righteous reasons, you need only to trust in the *Higher Power* and everything will be okay.

Line 6
The sixth line is *the belt was taken from one three times, even if that belt was momentarily bestowed upon him.* You can worry all you want about the conflict for as long as you want, and solve your problems on your own-but there will be consequences. If you just let go, then you will be victorious.

7. Shih - The Army

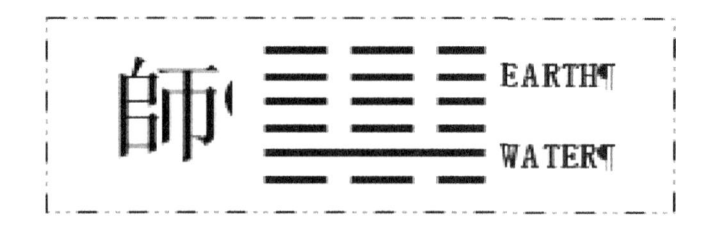

師 ☷ EARTH
☵ WATER

The representation

Judgment
At the head of an army is a leader. In times of war, the troops need someone to look up to-a man with strength and perseverance.

Image
Imagine a lake in the middle of the earth-water in the midst of dry land. That is an army, rolling and persevering even if there is nowhere else to go. By upholding generosity and understanding, the army will prevail.

Analysis

Conflict differentiates itself from war in that war is more perilous; it is a battle between one's self and the world. In times of war, a firm stance and an able leader are needed. Like that leader, you must not let others sway your decisions and principles. You must only "attack" or make a move when you feel that the time is right, when the *Higher Power* tells you so. In the same way, you must "retreat" or fall back when it is needed-do not let arrogance cloud your judgment.

Remember, while you are not alone, you must remain independent. Even during this time of battle, you must also remain neutral and fair. If you conduct yourself in the proper way, you will meet with success.

Line-by-line reading

Line 1
The first line is *an orderly army poised for battle.* Be ready. A battle is coming, and you must gather your bearings and ascertain that you are fighting for a just cause. If you are not ready, when the trials commence, you will find yourself at a loss.

Line 2
The second line is *one in the midst of an army.* Even if you are surrounded by others who may cause you to feel insecure or unsure, remind yourself to stay confident, yet humble. Ask the *Higher Power* for guidance.

Line 3
The third line is *the army carting off their fallen comrades in wagons*. Right now, you need to disengage yourself from the situation and retreat if you must. You have allowed yourself to be badly influenced; thus, you will only meet failure. Take a step back and breathe before continuing on your path.

Line 4
The fourth line is *an army in retreat*. Again, those who are inferior have wrongly influenced you. You must now disengage and retreat or meet with failure.

Line 5
The fifth line is *an animal to hunt in the middle of the field.* Catch it and hold on to it as you must hold on to your principles. Do not hastily rush into things or continue on the path you are now, lest you meet with failure.

Line 6
The sixth line is *the prince issuing commands and rewarding his people with lands.* If you proceed with humility, according to your

principles, then you will meet with success. If you become arrogant and hasty, you will meet with failure.

8. Pi - Holding Together (Union)

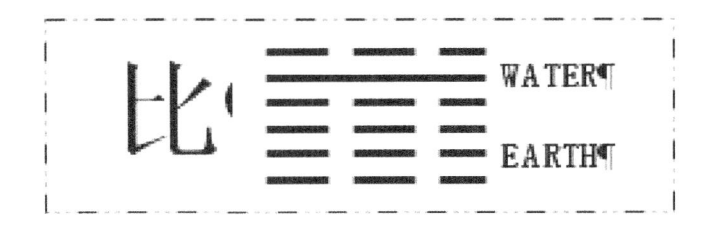

比 ☵ WATER
　 ☷ EARTH

The representation

Judgment
This oracle means you will meet with good fortune. Continue communing with the *Higher Power*, asking for guidance and help when it is necessary. Continue relying on your loved ones and asking them for help when necessary. With unity comes strength and success. Do not start too late.

Image
Imagine the waters and the earth working in harmony through the rain that nourishes the land. As a king works with his people to provide for the land, so should you work with those you care for to better your life.

Analysis

During this time, it is important that you make connections with others so that you can help each other work towards a common goal. An important part of unity is working together with the right attitudes-perseverance, truthfulness, and balance, among others.

Admittedly, all relationships are complicated-whether they be familial relations, friendships, or romantic attachments. Nevertheless, keep striving for unity and teamwork.

Line-by-line reading

Line 1
Right now, you need to act with honesty and loyalty in your heart. Your endeavors will be successful if you remain both honest and loyal to your teammates.

Line 2
Others will try to lead you astray. Persevere in acting with unity, honestly, and loyalty in all that you do.

Line 3
You may feel doubt and heaviness about your current endeavors. Make sure that you are working with the right people, who also endeavor to remain honest and loyal at all times.

Line 4
As much as inner perseverance is important, the attitude of your peers is important as well. They will be by your side when you do things; thus, you must learn to rely on those who will influence you in the right way.

Line 5
Do not attempt to impress or coerce people into befriending you. Follow the guidance of the *Sage* and you inner character will attract appropriate companions.

Line 6
When an opportunity comes to align yourself with a person of good will, act swiftly and wholeheartedly so that the moment will not be lost.

9. Hsiao Ch'u - The Taming Power Of The Small

小畜 — WIND / HEAVEN

The representation

Judgment
Small efforts are not insignificant. Right now, it is time for you to take small steps forward, cautiously proceeding and progressing. Do not make sudden lurches; just take it easy and take it slow. Even if you are having a hard time, small steps forward will bring you to where you need to go.

Image
Imagine the wind blowing through the heavens. The unseen wind can cause the clouds to move, trees to sway, and so much more. Small does not mean insignificant. Small things can have just as much impact as other things.

Analysis

Now is a time of turmoil. Thus, to make sure that you do not take a misstep, you need to take things slowly. Take small steps forward and relish whatever progress you achieve. While it may seem pointless, in the long run, you will find that the small steps you took today have defined your future.

Try to think of your current situation as the beginning of a season. The flowers are just budding and the leaves have just started turning green. Any sudden moves might disturb progress, so you must remain patient and persevering. If you feel the urge to do more and be more, curb that urge for the time being. Now is not the time.

Revel in the small steps, and you will eventually find yourself nearing the finish line.

Line-by-line reading

Line 1
The first line is *one returning to where he began.* Never forget your roots, and never forget your principles. Make sure to hold fast to them and do not be led astray.

Line 2
The second line is *one who returns willingly.* You may be feeling that now is not the time to act-listen to that feeling. Your decision of inaction will positively affect your efforts. Use this downtime to seek guidance from the *Higher Power*.

Line 3
The third line is *a rolling wheel whose spokes have broken and fallen away*. If you get tempted to take more than just a small step, you will be moving too fast. This will lead to your undoing.

Line 4
You need to stay upright in your beliefs; otherwise, you will fail. Do not resort to immoral methods; rather, stay patient and kind while slowly progressing towards your goal.

Line 5
If you stay true to your principles, those who are close to you will benefit as well. Loyalty and sincerity will serve you well.

Line 6
If you remain patient and continue abiding by your principles, then success is not far away. If you force progress and move too quickly, you will be taking steps backward. Your attitude will determine your success.

10. Lu - Treading (Conduct)

The representation

Judgment
If you tread carefully, you will be safe and successful. As always, hold fast to your principles while moving forward. You must remain upright in your dealings with your enemies, friends, and even yourself.

Image
Imagine the expanse between the heaven and the lake. You must know the difference between what is high and what is low-thus defining how you tread.

Analysis

You need not tread lightly, quickly, or carefully-you need only tread correctly, with the disposition of others in mind. The *I Ching* illustrates this point by saying, "Treading on the tail of the tiger. It does not bite the man." If you tread correctly, you will be able to overcome even the most impossible challenges.

In the same way, there is a prowling tiger within all of us that rears its head when we feel emotionally charged. Do not let yourself prowl and attack-instead, continue treading along the path you were meant to walk. Continue upholding perseverance, sincerity, honesty, and humility, among others. Only thus will you stay on the right path.

Line-by-line reading

Line 1
Simple conduct is desirable. Return to your basics and act according to what you feel is correct-do not complicate things.

Line 2
The second line is *one walking on an easy, level path.* Do not complain that you are not facing hardships-accept the blessing of an easy trek and keep moving.

Line 3
The third line is *a one-eyed man who sees and a lame man who treads on a tiger's tail-the man is bitten*. Do not force yourself to attempt anything wholly beyond your abilities because your ego is telling you to.

Line 4
The fourth line is *one treading on the tiger's tail who meets good fortune.* If you proceed carefully and with preparedness, you will achieve success.

Line 5
Even in the midst of trials, you must persevere in your patience and preparedness. In the same way, you need to let others tread their own paths. Be helpful, but do not spoon-feed those who approach you looking for help.

Line 6
The most important thing right now is that your conduct remain principled and morally correct. If you maintain good conduct, you will attract good fortune.

11. T'ai - Peace

泰 ☷ EARTH
☰ HEAVEN

The representation

Judgment
Peace is the beginning of greatness. Once you achieve peace, greatness, good fortune, and success will follow.

Image
Imagine the heavens becoming one with the earth. Peace reigns where there is equality and goodness. Conduct yourself with the right attitude and peace will follow.

Analysis

Don't let the small things bother you, because great things are about to happen. What is important is that you conduct yourself with dignity and civility-keep your principles close, making sure that you never stray from righteousness. It is important that you act and think with these principles in mind so that harmony, prosperity, and balance will be attracted to you.

Now is the best time to reach out and try new things, as good fortune will follow you. As long as you are innocent and balanced, you will meet with greatness. Do not forget your principles.

Line-by-line reading

Line 1

The first line is *uprooted grass with sod*. If you want to start something new, now is the time. You will meet good luck.

Line 2
You must remain neutral in your endeavors. When others treat you badly, respond with gentleness. If you meet with challenges, keep pushing forward, but maintain a neutral ground. Remember, even if things are peaceful and prosperous now, it will not always be so.

Line 3
The third line is *after all planes you will find a slope; after leaving, there is always a return*. After peace, tribulation will arise-accept the challenge with open arms without backing down. You will still have good fortune, so long as you remain true to yourself and the *Higher Power*.

Line 4
Though you are successful, remain humble, sincere, kind, and generous. Do not boast of your achievements; instead, share them with your neighbors. Do not pat yourself on the back; instead, stay sincere and considerate. Your actions will determine your luck.

Line 5
The *Higher Power* has something planned for you-believe it and wait patiently. Do not force yourself on a path that is not yours to take; it will end in disappointment. Rely on the guidance of the *Higher Power*, not your ego.

Line 6
The topmost line is *the walls falling back into the moat*. Peace does not last forever, but that is okay. Just trust in the *Higher Power* and keep moving forward. Resistance is futile, so accept the changing times and make the best of your situation.

12. P'i - Stagnation

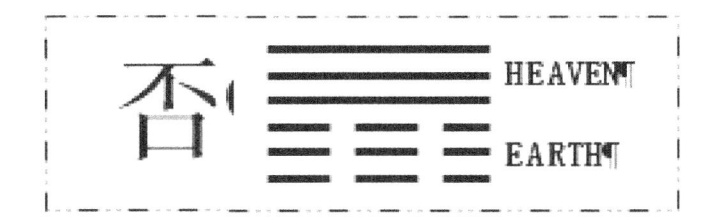

The representation

Judgment
This is the opposite of peace. Great times have just passed or are just about to come-but now is the time for acting small. This standstill should allow you to better yourself and your inner strength. It should also give you time to build a relationship with the *Higher Power*.

Image
Imagine the heaven and earth separating for good. Stagnation symbolizes a time of turmoil when the world is not in good shape. During this time, it would do you good to improve yourself rather than focus on the bad of the world.

Analysis

The separation of heaven from earth signifies that the *Higher Power* is far away from the people of this world. It means that chaos and misfortune are prevalent in society (e.g. unjust leaders, terrorist attacks, etc.).

During these times, do not let yourself be influenced by the world. Just because everyone is doing "it" does not mean you should do "it" too. At the same time, you should not let the stagnation of the world cause you to enter a state of stagnation yourself. Always be improving yourself. When the outside influencers are not good, look for influencers inside yourself and keep on making yourself better.

Line-by-line reading

Line 1
The first line is *uprooted grass with sod.* You hold no influence now, so do not try to change your surroundings. Instead, remain steadfast in your principles and do not let inferior influencers sway your actions.

Line 2
The stagnation gives you time to look into yourself and identify your inferior qualities. Bear with the hardships and stay strong, so that when the stagnation ends, you can rise to the occasion.

Line 3
Those who have done wrong will realize their wrongdoings and feel shame, but you must remain compassionate and neutral-no judgment should be found in you.

Line 4
Act with the guidance of the *Higher Power* and you can do no wrong. Your followers will share in your blessings, and your influence will grow.

Line 5
Conditions are now right for success-but you must still be careful if you are to achieve it. Leave nothing to chance; dot every "i" and cross every "t".

Line 6
Without the *Higher Power*, you will attain nothing-and God helps those who help themselves. As well as things are going now, they will not continue to do so without strenuous action on your part.

13. T'ung Jên - Fellowship With Men

The representation

Judgment
Creating successful relationships with others and maintaining those relationships embodies the principles required by the *Higher Power*. Let others see the *Sage's* goodness through you.

Image
Imagine the heavens uniting with fire. Just as the sun never fails to rise, so must we never fail to be a reliable party in any relationship.

Analysis

Never forget the sage advice of the *Higher Power*, especially when forming new relationships or maintaining old ones. This hexagram reminds us to keep our principles at the core of all our relationships, treating our friends, family, co-workers, partners, and others with respect, kindness, gentleness, and humility.

You must also make sure to keep only relationships that you can share with others. If you are embarrassed for any reason about maintaining a relationship with a certain person, then it is probably not right. If you remain righteous along with your companions, then you will achieve great things.

Line-by-line reading

Line 1

The first line is *one convening with others at the gate*. Make sure that your relationships are all out in the open. Doing otherwise will lead to your detriment.

Line 2
The second line is *one who gets along with his village and kin*. Do not show special, selfish consideration for those closest to you. Be friendly and kind to *everyone* so that you will be treated kindly in turn.

Line 3
The third line is *one hiding his weapon before climbing a hill-he does not progress for three years.* Lack of trust in your relationships will lead to your detriment. If you find yourself becoming paranoid, turn to the *Higher Power* for help.

Line 4
The fourth line is *one who climbs up a wall but does not attack*. Always consider the costs before picking a fight. Open conflict could ruin a relationship that might otherwise be salvaged in the future.

Line 5
The fifth line is *sorrowful men who have just been separated, but learn to laugh again after a while.* While separation may seem painful now, you will meet again and become happier. Do not let go of your relationships because of physical distance.

Line 6
The sixth line is *men who meet and bond in the meadow.* Your relationships need not be close or come with obvious benefits in order to be important. There is always value in companionship.

14. Ta Yu - Possession in Great Measure

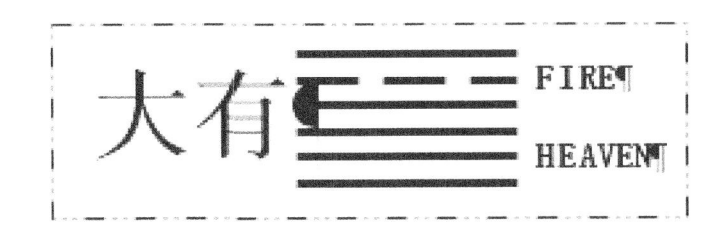

大有 ䷍ FIRE
HEAVEN

The representation

Judgment
You will receive a lot of blessings that will lead to your success.

Image
Imagine fire in heaven; this is the image of abundance. Even so, uphold righteousness and turn away from wrongdoing so that your blessings will keep coming.

Analysis

You are in perfect unity with the universe right now, and so you are experiencing a moment of plenty. If you uphold the principles of the *Sage*-kindness, gentleness, humility, and innocence, among others-your blessings will not end.

Even though you have achieved much, never let yourself become proud, for that will be your downfall. Also, remember to share your blessings with others as the *Sage* has gladly blessed you with more than you need. Be the good fortune that others will benefit from.

Line-by-line reading

Line 1
Although everything is running smoothly without effort on your part, you must not allow yourself to become arrogant or extravagant. Bear in mind that underlying issues must be resolved at some point.

Line 2
The second line is *a large empty wagon to carry things.* You have adequate resources, freedom, and assistance to advance your plans, and now is the time to make use of them.

Line 3
The third line is *an offering from a prince.* Do not hesitate to use your wealth and property for the good of all. Being too selfish will not further your cause.

Line 4
The fourth line is *a man who is unlike his neighbors.* In situations where you're the odd man out, it is especially important not to rock the boat.

Line 5
Be kind and straightforward while conducting yourself in an irreproachable manner, and you will enjoy great success.

Line 6
In many ways, you're on top of the world now. Just remember not to become too caught up with worldly things. Remain humble and keep following the path of the *Higher Power*.

15. Ch'ien - Modesty

謙 ☷ EARTH
☶ MOUNTAIN

The representation

Judgment
Modesty and reserve will lead to success.

Image
Imagine a green mountain on this earth, with just enough flora and fauna-that is the image of modesty. Life must be lived in the middle. Too much or too little of anything is bad.

Analysis

The *Higher Power* loves to assist those who remain modest despite their achievements and triumphs. Modesty means that you do not boast about your achievements. Rather, you should be thankful for having achieved what you have achieved and gained what you have gained. If you remain modest and thankful, you will achieve success. Listen not to your ego; rather, listen to your wit and the *Higher Power* and your current situation will definitely improve.

Line-by-line reading

Line 1
The first line is *one who is modest about his modesty*. Do not act entitled. Success once does not mean success forever. Remain humble and good fortune will follow you closely.

Line 2

The second line is *expressed modesty.* You are now experiencing a time of blessedness, but you must remain modest to maintain this state. Use these blessed times to reflect upon yourself and improve.

Line 3
The third line is *one who has achieved success through modesty and humility.* Through modesty and humility, you will continue to progress. If you stop to bask in the admiration of others, you will make a misstep and halt progress.

Line 4
Be sincere in your modesty. Do not announce it to the world and preach about your modesty. Rather, act how you must and bask in the knowledge that the *Higher Power* will reward you for your actions.

Line 5
The fifth line is *one who is humble before others.* In the face of others, remain humble but do not halt progress. Keep moving forward with the correct attitude.

Line 6
The sixth line is *expressed modesty.* Modesty expressed means upholding all that modesty stands for. It means turning away from feelings and values that are detrimental to one's well-being (e.g. pride and self-pity).

16. Yu - Enthusiasm

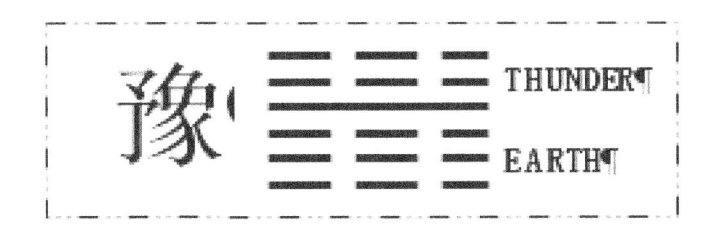

豫 THUNDER
　　 EARTH

The representation

Judgment
Now is the time to look for allies and to start moving. Enthusiasm will help you along.

Image
Imagine hearing the thunders of the skies coming from the earth itself. This is the image of enthusiasm; it is why ancient kings would bang drums to honor the heavens.

Analysis

According to the *I Ching*, there is a proper kind of enthusiasm. The enthusiasm fueled by the desires of the ego is the wrong kind of enthusiasm. Enthusiasm for chasing after worldly things will lead you nowhere. The proper kind of enthusiasm is guided by the *Higher Power* and will lead you to success. Let kindness and inner balance guide your enthusiasm so that you act in such a way that others will benefit as much as yourself.

Line-by-line reading

Line 1
The first line is *expressed enthusiasm*. Modesty and enthusiasm go hand in hand. While you are excited, you must not be boastful or unkind. Instead, focus on the guidance of the *Higher Power* and continue seeking the truth.

Line 2
The second line is *one stands who firm like a rock.* Even if others try to tell you otherwise, stand firm in your values and principles. Excitement that leads to wrongdoing will lead you astray.

Line 3
The third line is *enthusiasm and hesitation that lead to regret.* You know right from wrong-do not let peers convince you otherwise. Hesitating to do the right thing because others say so will lead to downfall.

Line 4
The fourth line is *where enthusiasm stems from.* Worry not, you are guided. Your friends will help you along the way, as will the *Higher Power*, as long as your sincerity remains.

Line 5
The fifth line is *one who is usually sick but does not pass from the world.* You can achieve success; you just need to stop getting in the way of it. Put your ego aside and practice proper enthusiasm.

Line 6
The sixth line is *one who is wrongly enthusiastic.* Reflect within yourself and understand that proper enthusiasm will bring you farther. Success is still possible, with correction.

17. Sui - Following

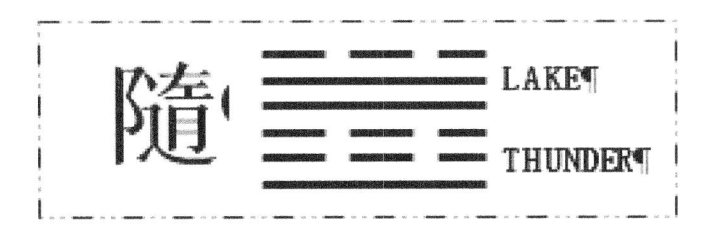

隨 ☱ LAKE
☳ THUNDER

The representation

Judgment
Following others and keeping an open mind will lead to your success. Persevere in your own ideals, but also make sure that you know when it is time to follow.

Image
Imagine thunder in the middle of the lake, the waters flowing outward while the sound waves follow them. This is the image of following. Now is not the time to lead, but to let others take the wheel.

Analysis

If you want others to follow you, you must first learn to follow those who lead. Do not try to break free from your current circumstances; rather, look around you and be content with what you have. Follow the ebb and flow of life for now, and do not try to manipulate it. Look into yourself and see what you have to improve rather than trying to change the way that things *are*. Only when you have achieved a certain acceptance will you be able to lead others rightly, with the *Higher Power* as your example.

Line-by-line reading

Line 1

The first line is *changing standards.* Changing standards is not always bad. Listen to those around you and change yourself accordingly. If you feel that you can improve yourself, do it.

Line 2
The second line is *one who clings to a young boy and thus loses strength.* You know more than the young boy-it does not benefit you to cling to inferiors.

Line 3
The third line is *one who clings to strength but loses a young boy.* The youth represents innocence. While you must not cling to the boy, you must not lose him entirely. Proceed with innocence and sincerity, without acting according to your ego.

Line 4
The fourth line is *success in following but failure in perseverance.* Following others will lead to your success, but if you persevere in trying to lead, you will fail. As always, uphold your values and you will not fail-but retain your following attitude.

Line 5
The fifth line is *sincerity that begets good luck.* Sincerity and innocence will bring you farther. Remember that your ego should not be entertained; rather, continue following with the sincerity of the *Sage*.

Line 6
The sixth line is *one whose followers are loyal.* You are the follower. Remember to remain loyal to the *Higher Power,* and he will guide you to your success. Following is what you must do right now.

18. Ku - Work On What Has Been Spoiled (Decay)

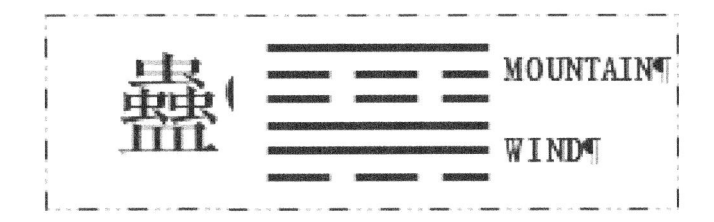

The representation

Judgment
Something is wrong with the way you are approaching things, but hope has yet to be lost. If you find what is wrong and work on yourself with the goal of improvement, you can still find success.

Image
The wind blowing the bottom of the mountains, leaving the peaks without its cold. This is the image of decay. Strengthen yourself and encourage improvement in those around you rather than giving up.

Analysis

This oracle means that you need to reflect upon yourself. You may be looking at things the wrong way, or reacting to them wrongly. Look into yourself and check if your values are still aligned with those of the *Sage*. If not, then you need to work on yourself and improve yourself accordingly. The first step to working on decay is identifying where it originates. After identifying the origin, you must spend time understanding it. After which, you must *remove it*. But your job is not done when the decay is gone. Your job is only done when you have ensured that it cannot return. You will only meet with success when you have reflected upon yourself and completely removed the decay.

Line-by-line reading

Line 1
The first line is *one who rights his father's wrongs.* Family tradition is, as the name suggests, *traditional*. But this does not mean that it is correct. If you know that your family has been doing wrong, change the tradition, for it benefits no one.

Line 2
The second line is *one who rights his mother's wrongs.* We tend to see our fathers' wrongs but love our mothers too much to see their wrongdoings. Look deep into yourself and your family, to truly see what is being hidden from you. When you find the decay, remove it, but in a gentle and loving manner.

Line 3
The third line is *one who rights his father's wrongs.* Even if it leads to conflict, you must find a way to right the wrongs in your immediate surroundings. Do not let decay go unnoticed; rather, cleanse yourself and those you care about, no matter the cost. Things will right themselves.

Line 4
The fourth line is *one who understands his father's wrongs.* Understanding and tolerating are two different things. You may *understand* what has been done wrong, but you *should not* tolerate it. Again, do not let decay take root-remove it from the get-go or suffer the consequences it brings.

Line 5
The fifth line is *one who rights his father's wrongs.* Just because something has been done wrong for many years *does not* mean you must play along. It is your job, as an enlightened being, to remove decay wherever you can. *Do not* inherit the wrongs of others-fight against them, and you will be rewarded with the praise of your peers.

Line 6

The sixth line is *one whose goals are higher than human superiority.* If you need a break from the world, by all means take it. Put some distance between yourself and wrongdoers so that you can improve yourself. Once you have improved yourself, you can better help the rest of the world.

19. Lin - Approach

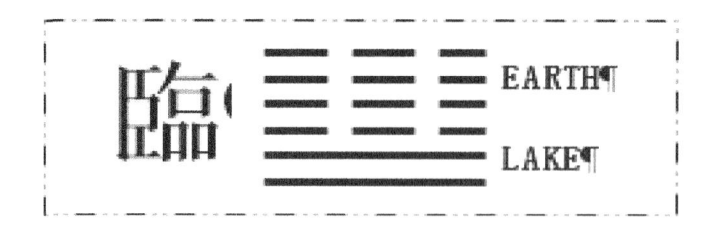

臨 ☷ EARTH
   ☱ LAKE

The representation

Judgment
Something is approaching and you must be prepared to greet it. An opportunity-and perhaps a danger-is nearing and you must be ready to accept it. If you approach it with the right attitude, you will meet with good fortune.

Image
Imagine the earth floating above a lake, receiving all nourishment therefrom. That is the image of approach. Something is coming-be prepared.

Analysis

Good is coming, but it will not be a smooth and easy path, and you must remain vigilant. Do not become relaxed in your principles; rather, hold them closer to your heart now more than ever. Good is approaching, and you must be prepared to meet it with both modesty and innocence. Remember too that you must greet both bad times and good times with acceptance, innocence, and humility, as the *Sage* has shown us. Do not relax your principles just because things are going well. Rather, practice them more vigorously so that when troubles inevitably strike, you will be ready.

Line-by-line reading

Line 1

The first line is *one who approaches with assistance.* The good times are beginning, but you must remain vigilant in your principles. Do not succumb to the temptations of your ego and desire.

Line 2
The second line is *one who approaches with assistance.* The good times are beginning, but you must look to the *Higher Power* and ask for guidance so that you will be prepared for all that is to come your way.

Line 3
The third line is *one who approaches comfortably.* Be comfortable in your success, but not complacent. Remember to be prepared for bad times by making ready during the good times.

Line 4
The fourth line is *one who approaches completely.* Others will try to help you-let them. Be open-minded rather than guarded. Accept the assistance of others when it is offered.

Line 5
The fifth line is *one who approaches wisely.* The *Higher Power* wants to help, but *He* can only help if you do not succumb to worldly things.

Line 6
The sixth line is *one who approaches with a great heart.* It is your task to guide others as the *Sage* guides you. Do not be selfish with your success-share it, but share it correctly by sharing principles and values, as well.

20. Kuan - Contemplation (View)

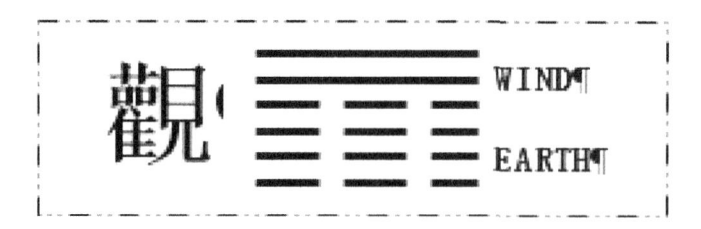

觀 ☴ WIND
☷ EARTH

The representation

Judgment
While you have cleansed yourself of wrongdoing, you have not yet completed the offering. Even so, your followers will continue to trust you.

Image
Imagine the wind slowly passing over fields, mountains, lakes, and the rest of the world. This is the image of contemplation. Just like the wind, a ruler must go over his domain and look to each of the sectors, understanding their needs and acting accordingly.

Analysis

This oracle means that you must contemplate yourself-your actions, thoughts, values, principles, and more-to be able to set an example for others. If you are true to yourself and to the principles that the *Sage* has taught you, then you will remain trustworthy and followed. If you are not, then you will meet with ruin. Carefully contemplate your current state and change yourself accordingly.

Line-by-line reading

Line 1
The first line is *one who contemplates like a child.* A child sees the world in black and white-what is true is good, what is false is bad. Just like a child, believe in the truth and lead others to believe in it,

as well; but as an adult, realize also that the world contains many shades of grey.

Line 2
The second line is *one who contemplates through a crack in the doorway.* You may not see the entire picture now, but you will in the future. The *Higher Power* has plans, and everything will fall into place. Contemplate what you know, and look forward to what is to come.

Line 3
The third line is *one who contemplates life.* Contemplate life, not as life itself, but as how *you* affect it. Your actions, thoughts, words, and values have affected life and what it has become. Take this time to contemplate life in general, and how you have affected it.

Line 4
The fourth line is *one who contemplates the light of the kingdom.* You will become a leader only if you are able to uphold values and discipline and lead others to do the same.

Line 5
The fifth line is *one who contemplates life.* Contemplate the good parts of life and learn to benefit yourself and others from the good rather than focusing on the bad.

Line 6
The sixth line is *one who contemplates his own life.* Contemplate on your actions and thoughts, cleansing them of evil. Remember to do your best to follow the examples that the *Sage* has left for us.

21. Shih Ho - Biting Through

噬嗑　FIRE / THUNDER

The representation

Judgment
You will meet with success when you take decisive action against obstructions. When challenges arise, they may be overcome with perseverance and the guidance of the *Higher Power*.

Image
Imagine the night sky filled with thunder and lightning. Just as these two come hand in hand, biting through will require you to work with others against those who would be obstacles to progress.

Analysis

The *I Ching* knows that you are going through challenges, and it advises that you act. Rather than looking inward, you must force the situation to change. Someone has broken the unity, and you need to make things right again. The rupture may have been caused by someone within your group, but remember also that it may be due to your own misconduct. *Do not* let go of your principles-they will save you, in the end. For now, bite through while relying on the *Higher Power* for guidance.

Line-by-line reading

Line 1
The first line is *one whose toes are securely fastened to stocks so that he does not lose them.* When you make a mistake, wallow not

in self-pity. Rather, learn from the mistake and take measures so that you do not make it again.

Line 2
The second line is *one who bites into meat so eagerly that you cannot see his nose.* If you stray from the truth, you will meet with adversity. Do not be overzealous; rather, remain humble and calm.

Line 3
The third line is *one who eats old meat and thus gets poisoned.* Rather than let yourself get poisoned, withdraw from an argument. It does not make you weak; rather, it makes you strong enough to see that peace is better than lasting discord.

Line 4
The fourth line is *one who eats seemingly rotten meat.* Stand firm on middle ground. Do not relax your principles. Stay strong in your beliefs and you will find that you are alright.

Line 5
The fifth line is *one who eats dried, lean meat.* Trust in the *Higher Power*, that *He* will make sure that you are safe. Do not stray from your path and join with others who do not uphold the same values. Rather, be patient and strive to stay in the middle so that you will not fail

Line 6
The sixth line is *one whose neck has been fastened to a cangue, whose ears have disappeared.* Do not stubbornly persist in what you know to be wrong. You will ultimately fail. Stay alert to the nudging of the *Sage*. Through holding steadfast to *His* principles, you will meet with success.

22. Pi - Grace

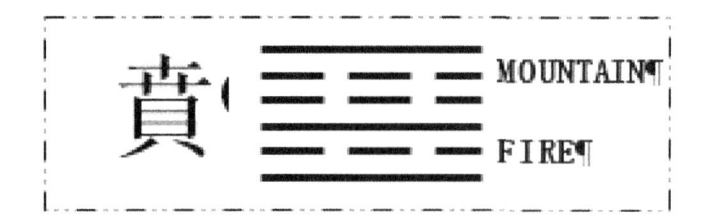

賁 ☶ MOUNTAIN
☲ FIRE

The representation

Judgment
Acting with grace will lead you to success in small tasks. If you have plans, it is time to act.

Image
Imagine fire at the foot of the mountain, neither spreading nor climbing. This is the image of grace, as the mountain remains calm and poised in the face of danger. Remember to deal with problems with grace and clarity.

Analysis

You must hold yourself with gentleness and kindness. Whatever you are going through right now, you need to remember that your values reflect upon yourself and the *Sage*. Listen to *Him*. While it is easier to become impatient and try to manipulate situations, a gentle and calm mind will help bring you closer to your goal by small, seemingly insignificant steps. Trust that everything wall fall into place if you handle the situation with both grace and composure.

Line-by-line reading

Line 1
The first line is *one who places grace in his toes*. Tread carefully and follow those who have walked the path before. Heed not your arrogance, because it will lead to your failure.

Line 2
The second line is *one who places grace in his beard.* Do not put up false appearances; rather, stay true to yourself and learn the truth about others.

Line 3
The third line is *one who is both graceful and positive.* Grace under pressure is important, but grace during good times is just as important. However, even though things are going well, do not become complacent.

Line 4
The fourth line is *one who is distraught between gracefulness and simplicity.* Remain graceful and modest so that you will meet success. Do not try to manipulate the situation or force something else to happen.

Line 5
The fifth line is *hills and gardens that are peaceful and graceful.* Do not listen to your ego; luxury and material possessions are important to society, but not to the *Higher Power*.

Line 6
The sixth line is *grace in simplicity.* Grace is not weakness-it is strength. Knowing when to act and how to act is a gift that few possess. Seek true power from the guidance of the *Sage* instead of false power that is manipulated by the world.

23. Po - Splitting Apart

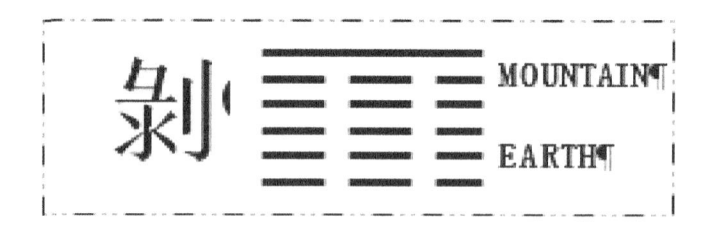

剝 ☷ MOUNTAIN
   ☷ EARTH

The representation

Judgment
While things are falling apart, do not enact new plans. Listen to the *Higher Power* and remain calm where you are. Now is *not* the time to act.

Image
Imagine all the mountains on the face of the earth, neither moving nor growing. There remains a divide between the peak and the foot of the mountain, as there is in society, but if you give to those in need, bridging the gap, you will meet with success.

Analysis

Do not act. It is important that you do not interfere with the inferior powers at play. While it may *seem* smarter to act now and react as quickly as possible-it is not. Accept your situation and cling to the *Higher Power* for guidance. Do not get entangled with those inferior to you because you *will* lose and you will be unsuccessful. Things will right themselves if you act correctly, hold steadfast in your principles, and trust that inaction is better than anything you can do.

Line-by-line reading

Line 1
The first line is *the broken leg of the bed.* While you are on unsteady ground, do not attempt to resolve the situation. Such actions are

propelled by fear, doubt, and your ego, and will be ineffective.

Line 2
The second line is *the broken edge of the bed.* Trouble is drawing closer, but cautiousness and patience remain the order of the day. Foolhardiness will lead to injury and failure.

Line 3
The third line is *one who splits with others.* Remain steadfast in your beliefs even when others tell you otherwise. Remove yourself from those who try to lead you astray.

Line 4
The fourth line is *the broken skin of the bed.* While your troubles may seem overwhelming now, stay calm and composed. Look into yourself and reflect on how you can improve rather than wallowing in your troubles or trying to resolve them.

Line 5
The fifth line is *a school of fish.* Imagine a school of fish turning around, all the fish moving in one coordinated motion to head in a different direction. If you correct your attitude, you will be able to effect such a drastic change as well.

Line 6
The sixth line is *a large, uneaten piece of fruit.* After a while, that fruit will decay. If you place it near other fruit, the other fruit will decay, as well; but if you place it on fertile ground more fruit will grow from its seeds. Likewise, good and evil will spread according to your actions. Stay strong in your convictions and you will be fine.

24. Fu - Return (The Turning Point)

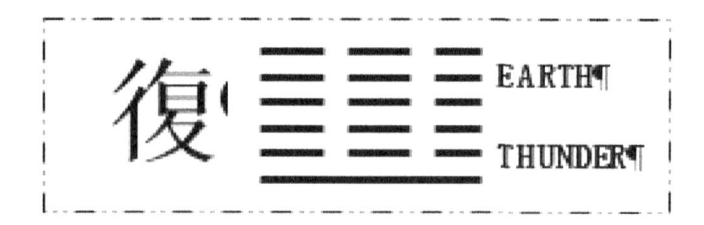

復 ☷ EARTH ☳ THUNDER

The representation

Judgment
Fu symbolizes a return to the light. Friends will come back, success will return, and bad things will leave your life. Now is the time to continue what has been left behind.

Image
Imagine the thunder *inside* the earth. This is the image of return. It is a turning point, of sorts, a climax after which things will finally turn for the better.

Analysis

This oracle means that you are on the way back to the light. Goodness will surround you and success will be close at hand. But you should not become egotistical or overconfident, for these will lead to your downfall. Treat your friends correctly and share your blessings with them. Thank the *Higher Power* for giving you such a bountiful harvest. And above all, remain true to your principles and follow the example of the *Sage* so that your abundance will continue to flow.

Line-by-line reading

Line 1
The first line is *one returning from a short journey.* While it is hard to stay completely on the path of good, straying will lead to downfall.

Be careful where you tread, and make sure your intentions remain pure.

Line 2
The second line is *one who returns quietly.* Do not let pride guide your steps. Do not disdain to follow in the footsteps of others, or to invite them to your table to share your good fortune.

Line 3
The third line is *one who returns repeatedly.* Perseverance is needed if you want to remain in good fortune. Do not be hasty and try to manipulate the path. If you stray, come back as many times as necessary.

Line 4
The fourth line is *one who returns alone after walking with others.* If others are dragging you down, turn to the *Sage* for guidance, for *He* is the only one whose opinions matter.

Line 5
The fifth line is *one who returns with dignity.* Even if you have erred, you need not despair. Return with your head held high, acknowledging that you have done wrong and promising that you will make amends.

Line 6
The sixth line is *one who misses the return.* Do not waste this opportunity because you do not want to change your ways. Look inward and identify what you can improve rather than blaming others for your misfortunes.

25. Wu Wang - Innocence (the Unexpected)

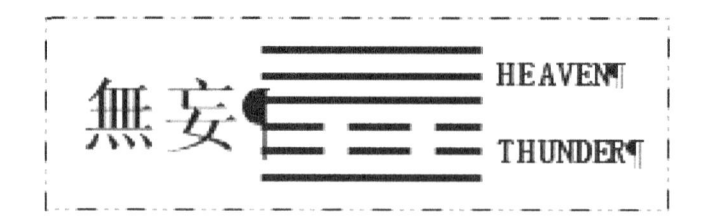

無妄 ═══ HEAVEN
      ═ ═ THUNDER

The representation

Judgment
Act like the innocents do and you will meet with success. If you go against your nature, you will meet with failure.

Image
Imagine thunder booming in the skies, as the rain pours and cleanses the earth. That is the image of innocence. Innocence will lead to good fortune and correct conduct.

Analysis

All of us have innocence within us-a pure and white light that struggles to remain free. Human nature stifles the light, making us go against our natural inclination to remain innocent. Thus, we must strive harder to hold on to that innocence and let it lead us. Let go of ego and negative emotions. Actions that are influenced by negative emotions will lead to failure. When you have difficulty in accessing that innocence, turn to the *Higher Power* and *He* will guide you in whatever you need to do.

Line-by-line reading

Line 1
The first line is *innocence that brings success.* Detach yourself from the world and its temptations. Remain innocent and success will follow you.

Line 2
The motivation behind your actions must not be the end result or the prize that you will gain. Rather, do what needs to be done, when it needs to be done, and you will meet with success.

Line 3
The third line is *misfortune that was wrongly placed.* While this misfortune is not your fault, it is imperative that you accept it and move forward. Wallowing in self-pity will not get you anywhere. Progress is led by acceptance and wisdom. The *Higher Power* will guide you.

Line 4
The fourth line is *one who perseveres.* Others will always try to sway you from doing what is right. Innocence is a light that many want to snuff out-do not let them.

Line 5
Disengage from misfortunes that are not of your own doing. Remain innocent and believe that things will right themselves, and you will escape your troubles unharmed.

Line 6
Live sincerely, without any ulterior motives. Even if your circumstances seem hopeless, your goal unattainable, quietly accept your fate and keep going. Do not try to force an impossible situation to occur, lest you lose your innocence.

26. Ta Ch'u - The Taming Power of the Great

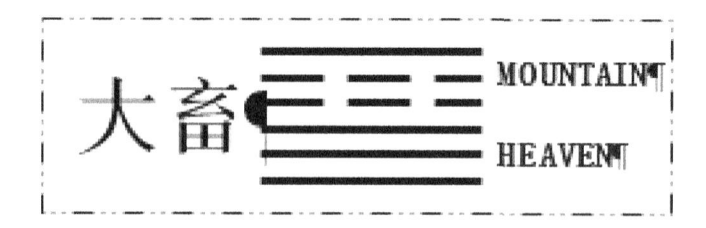

大畜 — MOUNTAIN / HEAVEN

The representation

Judgment
In times like this, turn to the *I Ching* for guidance. While something great is brewing, you must stay calm, persevere, and act to the best of your abilities-you will get through it.

Image
Imagine a mountain reaching the heavens. Just as the peak has reached the heavens, you will meet with success through wisdom, effort, and perseverance.

Analysis

Opposition can never be completely eliminated, but the way you handle these challenges will direct the outcomes. The power of the great can only be found in the *Higher Power,* and during times of tribulation, it is in your best interest to turn to *Him.* While you may think that testing all that you have learned from the *I Ching* is a smart course of action, it is not. You must not let yourself get tempted into attacking your opposition. Rather, keep a calm mind and hold your values close to yourself so that you do not lose them. Meet opposition with principled strength and the detachment of one who is ready to put his faith in the *Sage.*

Line-by-line reading

Line 1

The first line is *one who is in danger.* While you may believe that rushing into things and reacting now will yield results, it will *not.* Power through challenges with restraint and patience, and you will succeed.

Line 2
The second line is *axles that are taken from the cart.* Even if you struggle to advance, you will get nowhere. Accept your fate and look within yourself, constantly honing your skills. Do not strike until the time is right.

Line 3
The third line is *a horse that follows its master.* Do not mind those who are inferior to you, but be prepared to defend yourself from their attacks and stand firm in the values that the *I Ching* has taught you. Through this, you will meet with success.

Line 4
The fourth line is *a young bull with its headboard.* Do not let your emotions direct your line of action. Take a step back, clear your head, and then act to prepare yourself for future threats.

Line 5
The fifth line is *the tusk of a castrated boar.* Strong desire will lead you astray. Desire is a quality of which you must rid yourself. Practice neutrality and the rest will fall into place.

Line 6
The sixth line is *one who has stayed true to the principles of the Higher Power.* Your steadfastness will be rewarded. There are no obstacles in your way, because you have chosen to follow what is right.

27. I - The Corners of the Mouth (Providing Nourishment)

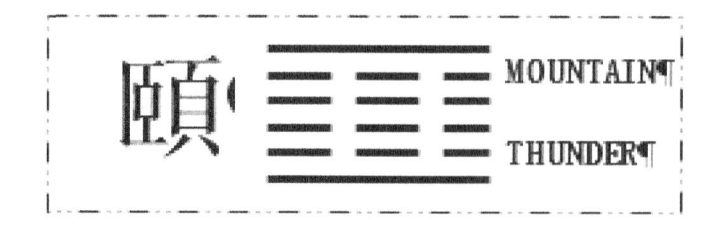

颐 — MOUNTAIN / THUNDER

The representation

Judgment
While food is nourishment for the body, meditation and communing with the *Higher Power* are nourishment for the soul. Persevere in righteousness and provide nourishment for both your body *and* soul.

Image
Imagine thunders booming at the base of a mountain. This is the image of providing nourishment. Before climbing, a man will think about what he will say, what he will bring to eat and drink, and what he still needs to prepare.

Analysis

Nourishment is important-for both the body and the soul. It will do you good to take in nourishment for your soul by reading the *I Ching* and surrounding yourself with others who can also provide nourishment. Inspect others by observing how they nourish themselves and those around them. Through stripping yourself of desires (or keeping them at a minimum), communing with the *Sage* daily through meditation, and upholding tranquility in all that you do, you will meet with success.

Line-by-line reading

Line 1

The first line is *one who has become saddened by the loss of his magic turtle.* Do not give in to the negative emotions of doubt and envy. Doubt and envy will force you to rely on others-do not let this happen.

Line 2
The second line is *one who has strayed from the path to get a drink of water.* Do not stray from the path to meet with one who is lazy-they will not provide you ample nourishment and will drag you down with them.

Line 3
The third line is *one who shuns nourishment.* Chasing after what you desire may seem like nourishment, but it is not. It is the exact opposite. Detach yourself from the world before it starts stealing nourishment from you.

Line 4
The fourth line is *one who looks for nourishment at the summit.* If you nourish yourself, you will reach the peak and be able to attract others to help you in your endeavors.

Line 5
The fifth line is *one who has strayed from the path.* Something is holding you back and getting you lost. Turn to those you trust, or the *Sage,* to guide your next steps.

Line 6
The sixth line is *one who is the source of nourishment.* Emulating the *Sage* and bringing others to nourishment will bring you great good fortune.

28. Ta Kuo - Preponderance of the Great

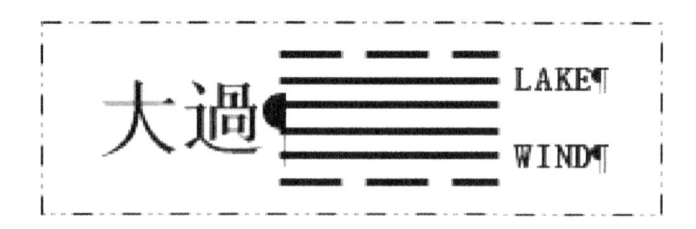

```
━━━━━  ━━━━━   LAKE
━━━━━━━━━━━
大過    ━━━━━━━━━━━
━━━━━━━━━━━
━━━━━━━━━━━   WIND
━━━━━  ━━━━━
```

The representation

Judgment
The fishing pole bends, almost to the point of snapping. Turn away and make other plans, and you will find success.

Image
Imagine the lake rising above the trees and the wind. This is the image of preponderance of the great. Think not of the world and its woes and troubles; focus first on yourself before helping others.

Analysis

The pressure on you right now is only getting stronger-but if you succumb to your base desires you will snap under pressure. This moment is one for which you have been preparing for quite some time now, but you never truly understand how hard it is to stay graceful under pressure until that moment is breathing down your neck. Strengthen yourself by heeding the teachings of the *Higher Power* and by holding steadfast in your principles. They will guide you to the light. Look into yourself and steel yourself for what is to come. If you remain strong yet humble, you will meet with success.

Line-by-line reading

Line 1
The first line is *one who spreads white rushes all over a field.* When starting something new, the foundation is always the most important

part. Without a strong base, the building will crumble.

Line 2
The second line is *an old man marrying a young woman and a new plant sprouting where one has dried.* However unlikely it seems, growth and progress is coming. You need to encourage this growth while remaining humble and reflective.

Line 3
The third line is *a ridgepole that is near breaking point.* Do not force yourself to manipulate the situation. Rather, keep moving forward at a slow pace, taking great care in your steps.

Line 4
The fourth line is *a ridgepole that has been reinforced.* Holding onto your principles and working with others leads to a strong foundation. You will not snap, and you will help others proceed. Remain humble and you will not fail.

Line 5
The fifth line is *an old woman marrying a young man and a withered plant mysteriously blooming.* You have started building on a weak foundation. Do not continue, or everything will be for naught.

Line 6
The sixth line is *one who crosses the waters and allows them to consume him.* When you must act for the good, you should do so without regard for the consequences to yourself. Always turn to the *Higher Power* for sound advice and guidance.

29. K'an - the Abysmal (Water)

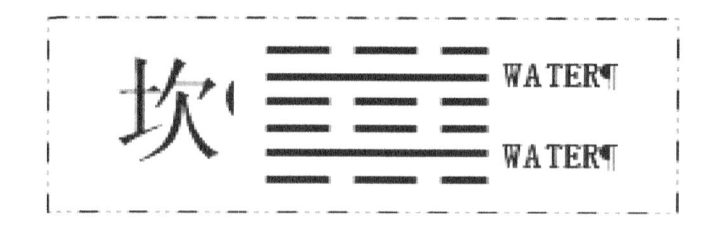

The representation

Judgment
While danger has returned, you must accustom yourself to the situation and remain true to your values in order to meet with success.

Image
Imagine flowing water-water flowing to the end, to its final destination. This is the image of the Abysmal. Remember to stay true to your values, and teach others of these values.

Analysis

No matter what hardships block your path, if you flow around them like the waters from the heavens, you will meet a just end. If you are looking for an easy solution to your problems, stop this course of action; it will lead to your failure. Do not let your negative emotions spur you into action. Rather, choose your course of action based on the nudging of the *Higher Power*. Do not fall into comfort and desire- turn away from these worldly temptations. Like the water, prepare yourself for challenges, but flow over them with strength, determination, humility, and innocence.

Line-by-line reading

Line 1

The first line is *one who falls into the abyss.* Bad habits will lead you astray. Rid yourself of them before you fall into a dark pit with no hope of climbing back up.

Line 2
The second line is *a dangerous pit.* There is a nasty, dark fall right in front of you that you must avoid. Turn to the *Higher Power* for guidance, and take only small steps. Patience is key.

Line 3
The third line is *an eternal abyss.* Everywhere you look, you will see darkness and the abyss, because right now is not a time for action. Stay calm and look within yourself. Wait patiently until a clear path presents itself.

Line 4
The fourth line is *a bowl of rice served with wine.* The *Higher Power* is more than willing to help you. Although such assistance may come in humble form, with *Him* by your side, you will get through your trials.

Line 5
The fifth line is *an abyss filled to the brim.* Do not force a solution to present itself-whatever arises will be incorrect. Rather, turn away from ambition and hold on to patience. Wait for a solution to present itself before taking the next step.

Line 6
The sixth line is *one who is tied and trapped in a prison.* Your conscience will tell you what is right and what is wrong-if you disobey your conscience, you will get trapped in your own wrongdoings. Ignoring your impulses will free you from the traps.

30. Li - The Clinging, Fire

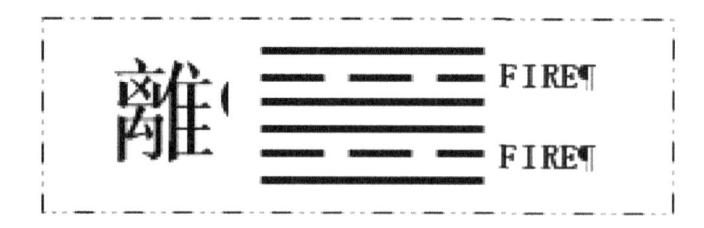

离 ☲ FIRE
☲ FIRE

The representation

Judgment
Care for those who care and provide for you, and you will meet success. Cling to those who provide benefits and persevere to provide for others as well.

Image
Imagine the brightness of rising twin flames. This is the image of clinging. By clinging to what is good and encouraging the flames, one can spread light to the world.

Analysis

Clinging to good principles and sound judgment is the best course of action. Even if you feel impatient for lack of progress, focusing on yourself and how you can help others is more important. Cling to those who provide nourishment to your soul as food nourishes your body, and you will find that you are progressing more than you realize. Being dependent is the natural inclination of human beings. Do not shun this inclination-embrace it and make it work for you. Cling to the *Higher Power* and people who will give you nourishment.

Line-by-line reading

Line 1

The first line is *intersecting footprints.* Walk sure-footedly and slowly so that you will not need to double back.

Line 2
The second line is *a yellow-hued light.* Remember that moderation is key. Be both despairing and enthusiastic-but just enough of each so that you remain balanced.

Line 3
The third line is *a setting sun to which young men rejoice and the old cry.* Do not complain about beginnings and ends that are inevitable. Rather, do what you can with your time and rejoice in your current situation.

Line 4
The fourth line is *something that suddenly appears.* Progress that comes too quickly will not last long. Lasting progress comes from continual dependence on the nourishment of the *Higher Power* rather than happenstance or strenuous effort.

Line 5
The fifth line is *a flood of tears.* Recognizing the futility of earthly pleasures may be difficult and depressing, but it is a good and necessary step on the path to enlightenment. Disengage yourself from your ego and act with your heart.

Line 6
The sixth line is *one is used to reprimand, killing off the leaders.* Self-acceptance and modesty are keys to a better course of action. Do not let your minor failings discourage you; rather, remove those that are most harmful and focus on your positive traits.

31. Hsien - Influence (Wooing)

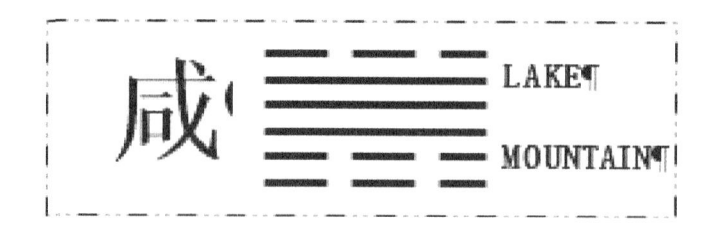

The representation

Judgment
Influencing others will lead to success. Believe in your abilities and embrace what is new-do not let others cloud your judgment.

Image
Imagine a lake on the mountain, providing nourishment to all its inhabitants. This is the image of influence. When others approach, do not hesitate to listen to their advice.

Analysis

As always, persevere in your principles. A surprising influence is coming, and you are to greet it. Your manner of greeting will dictate how things progress. Whatever this influence is-a message from the *Higher Power*, the appearance of a friend, an unexpectedly sad event-you need to meet it with both grace and acceptance. Act correctly and you will be rewarded accordingly.

Line-by-line reading

Line 1
The first line is *the influence found in the big toe.* Your toe is in the door; it's time to get your foot in. Remember to look into yourself and reflect upon your principles. Remove the things that need to be removed and improve what needs to be improved.

Line 2
The second line is *the influence found in the calves.* Patience is key to progress. Do not be influenced by others who will strive to turn you from your path. Remain patient and persevering.

Line 3
The third line is *the influence found in the thighs.* Rushing into things will lead you to ruin. Calm yourself and keep yourself still. Contemplate things before acting.

Line 4
The fourth line is *a conflicted man to whom only his friends are willing to listen.* Again, remain still and calm in your current state. Leave behind all your negative emotions-ambition and desire included.

Line 5
The fifth line is *the influence found in the nape.* Listen to the *Higher Power* and avoid being manipulated by those around you. Adapt to your situation and accept your state rather than trying to change it.

Line 6
The sixth line is *the influence found in the cheek, jaws, and tongue.* Do not use your words to share what you have learned. Rather, become a living testament of the teachings of the *I Ching.* Show others the proper path.

32. Hêng - Duration

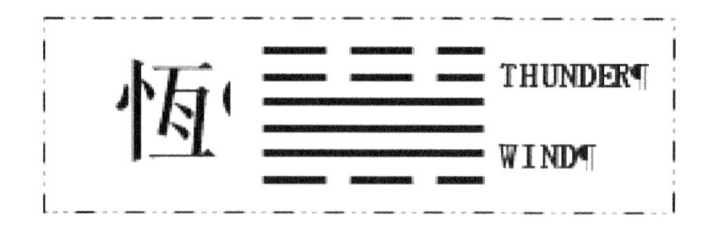

恆 THUNDER
WIND

The representation

Judgment
Perseverance will bring you to where you need to be. Even if the journey is long, it will be worth it. Perseverance will lead you to success.

Image
Imagine standing against the thunder and the wind. This is the image of Duration. Whatever challenges come your way, know that you need to persevere and hold steadfast in your commitments.

Analysis

Remain constant in your path and you will meet with success. This oracle means that you are currently treading the right path-do not stray. This is the right way, and you must stay on it. Do not move too fast, desire too much, or get tempted to change course. Hold your principles close to your heart and keep on walking.

Line-by-line reading

Line 1
The first line is *one who is moving too fast and persistently*. Good things come to those who wait. Do not expect progress to happen instantly.

Line 2

The second line is *disappearing remorse.* Rely on your principles to control your inner strength so that you do not overextend yourself. Disengage from your ego and you will be fine.

Line 3
The third line is *one who has abandoned his principles.* Do not let others change who you are. Stay on your path. Getting swayed by others will lead to misfortune.

Line 4
The fourth line is *an empty field.* To achieve your goals you must approach them at the correct time and place. Do not let your ambition cloud your judgment.

Line 5
The fifth line is *one persevering in his principles.* Tread your path without straying, but be ready to adapt to circumstances. Let others be and allow them to find their own ways as you have found yours.

Line 6
The sixth line is *one who is restless instead of patient.* Restlessness will lead to ruin. Do not let impatience get in the way of a happy ending.

33. Tun - Retreat

```
遯  ═══════  HEAVEN
    ═══════
    ═══ ═══  MOUNTAIN
```

The representation

Judgment
Knowing when to turn back will lead to success. Retreating is not always bad-sometimes it is needed in preparation for the greater battles. Small acts and perseverance will guide you.

Image
Imagine a mountain thrusting up under the heavens. This is the image of retreat. The heavens do not stay to meet the thrust; rather, they evade it by pulling away out of reach.

Analysis

Knowing when to retreat is an important part of life. Just as a flower cannot grow in the winter, you must not try to become prosperous during a time of scarcity. It is better if you take a step back and let nature take its course. Mind you, retreating does not mean giving up. It just means waiting for better circumstances and improving oneself before taking that next step.

Line-by-line reading

Line 1
The first line is *one who is retreating with his tail between his legs.* You are retreating too late. Do not wait until you have no choice but to retreat. Retreat while you still have hope for riding out the coming storm.

Line 2
The second line is *one who is bound with ox hide.* While retreating, stand firm with your friends and uphold your beliefs and values so that you will find a better path.

Line 3
The third line is *an interrupted retreat.* Cling to truth so that you may retreat with success. If you let others dissuade you, your retreat will not be so peaceful or successful.

Line 4
The fourth line is *a willing retreat.* Sometimes, continuing the fight will only weaken you and strengthen your opponent. In these times, you need to remove yourself and reflect.

Line 5
The fifth line is *a friendly retreat.* Retreat so that you may uphold righteousness in your heart. Be friendly, but do not let your inferiors influence your way of thinking.

Line 6
The sixth line is *a cheerful retreat.* The path to success will become clear once you master your ego and commit to a retreat for the time being.

34. Ta Chuang - the Power of the Great

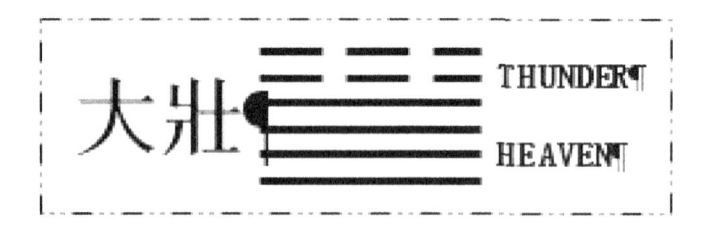

大壯 ☳ THUNDER
☰ HEAVEN

The representation

Judgment
Perseverance will bring you farther, as the Power of the Great will guide you and yours-so long as you act in accord with the principles of the *Higher Power*.

Image
Imagine the thunder from the heavens, announcing that the heavens hear. This is the image of the Power of the Great. Do not stray from the path that the *Higher Power* has led you to take.

Analysis

Remaining steadfast in your principles and the principles that the *Sage* has taught you is key to your inheritance of great power. There are many ways to attain power-but only power attained with good intentions truly lasts and matters. Do not let your ego guide you to obtain temporary power. Let your good nature present you with true power.

Line-by-line reading

Line 1
The first line is *power found in the toes.* You have false power, attained by the guidance of the ego. Rid yourself of this and right your path.

Line 2
Modesty and gentleness will lead you to the proper path. You will find your opposition starting to crumble. Let humility guide in your next steps and shove aside overconfidence.

Line 3
The third line is *an inferior abusing power and a superior who disapproves.* If you rush headfirst into something, you will only injure yourself. Avoid inferiors who will counsel you to act with foolhardiness.

Line 4
The fourth line is *a clearing in the hedges.* Though the work may be slow, carefully removing your obstacles is the right way to go about it. Do not make a show of it, but work quietly and with purpose.

Line 5
The fifth line is *one who has lost a goat.* Stubbornness and hardheadedness will lead to your demise. Listen now and be guided.

Line 6
The sixth line is *a goat stuck in a hedge.* Your struggles will worsen your predicament and you will never get free. Acceptance, reflection and improvement will be keys to your success.

35. Chin - Progress

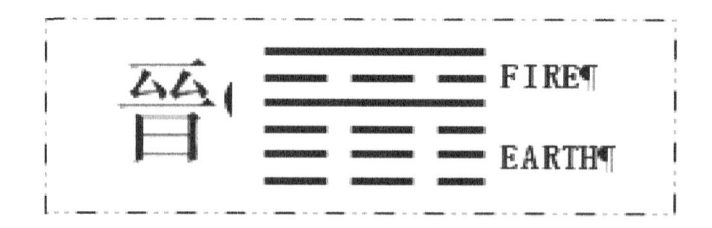

```
晋    ═══ ═══ ═══  FIRE
      ═ ═ ═ ═ ═ ═  EARTH
```

The representation

Judgment
With the help of the *Higher Power*, all things are possible. Progress will be made inevitable. You will receive plenty, if only you learn to listen to the *Sage*.

Image
Imagine a ball of fire rising over the earth-the sun. As the sun progresses over the earth, so will you so long as you remain on the bright path.

Analysis

You are met with great progress and fortune. Right now, it will be easy for you to make progress in your endeavors. Proceed with the guidance of the *Sage* and your principles, and you will be alright. Remember, though, that during times of progress and plenty, it is easier to fall into a boastful state. Do not let yourself be led by your ego, lest you halt your progress and lose the opportunity.

Line-by-line reading

Line 1
The first line is *one who has turned away in the midst of progress*. Even if you are plagued by a lack of confidence, continue on your path. Remain righteous and you will meet success.

Line 2
The second line is *one who is unhappy with his progress.* Do not let temporary setbacks deter you. Carry on, and in good time you will receive your just reward from the appropriate source.

Line 3
The third line is *a united village.* Everyone has their shortcomings-do not complain about yours. Others who are like you will come forward to assist you in your plight.

Line 4
The fourth line is *progress likened to a hamster.* Incorrect conduct may bring initial success, but your misdeeds will catch up with you if you persist in them. If you let your ego lead, that will be what becomes of you. Rather, stay humble and unselfish and success will follow.

Line 5
The fifth line is *disappearing remorse.* Do not be discouraged by each loss, and do not rejoice for each gain. Rather, disengage yourself and observe so that you may see the bigger picture.

Line 6
The sixth line is *progress by harsh methods is only allowed for self-improvement.* Do not force others to do your bidding or assist you through harsh and hurtful means. Rather, focus that harshness inward to improve yourself and correct your errors.

36. Ming I - Darkening of the Light

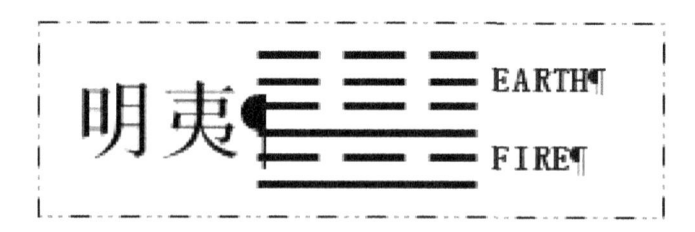

明夷 ䷣ EARTH / FIRE

The representation

Judgment
Even as the night falls, one must remain steadfast in his commitments and values. Face challenges with the help of the *Higher Power*.

Image
Imagine the ball of fire disappearing under the earth. This is the image of the Darkening of the Light. Even in the darkness, if you retain a light within yourself, you will meet with success.

Analysis

In times of darkness, you need to maintain your light by holding your principles close. Look to the *Higher Power* for guidance and help. Do not interact with those who will influence you wrongly; rather, contemplate upon yourself and keep to yourself. If you keep your principles close, you will still make progress, albeit slowly.

Line-by-line reading

Line 1
The first line is *the light disappearing while one is flying.* You cannot run away from your problems, but even though there will be hardships along the way, you must keep your destination firmly in mind. Turn to the *Higher Power* for and do not let your light go out.

Line 2

The second line is *the disappearing light has caused one to hurt his left thigh.* If you succumb to the darkness around you, it will wound you. Treat your injury by helping others who have also been injured.

Line 3
The third line is *the sun setting while men are out hunting.* Identifying the source of the problem does not mean that it will be instantly solved. Persevering in correctness and patience will get you to that solution.

Line 4
The fourth line is *one who has had the left side of his stomach run through.* In the time of darkness, any negativity can influence you badly. Reflect within yourself and remove all negative influencers.

Line 5
The fifth line is *the light retreats with Prince Chi.* There is no more light to be found in your surroundings. Look for light within yourself and hold on to it.

Line 6
The sixth line is *darkness.* Darkness is everywhere and it is at its strongest. Remember that this will not be a permanent state, and find light within yourself so that you will not succumb to it.

37. Chia Jên - the Family (Clan)

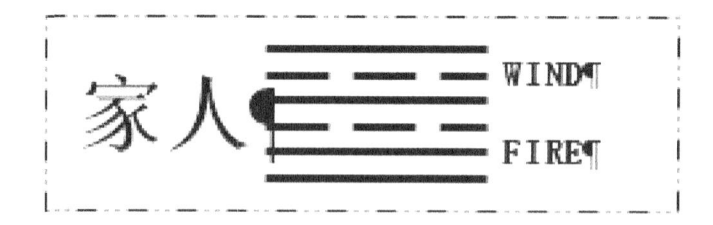

家人 ䷤ WIND / FIRE

The representation

Judgment
In the family, a woman's perseverance will go a long way. Man and woman must work together to make the home, but when the man falls short, the woman must persevere.

Image
Imagine the wind coming from the fire. This is the image of family. As the wind feeds the fire, parents must nourish their families through integrity and right conduct.

Analysis

The family is the smallest unit of any society. And every unit needs at least one enlightened leader. The *I Ching* tells us that we need to improve ourselves so that we can do good by those around us. When we uphold our principles and lead others to the *Higher Power*, we become successful in upholding relationships and familial ties.

Line-by-line reading

Line 1
The first line is *one who keeps to his family*. The family must be disciplined. Giving in to the ego is never the correct path.

Line 2
The second line is *one who gives in to her wants*. Do not aggressively reprimand; rather, use reasoning and gentleness to

sway others.

Line 3
The third line is *uncontrolled tempers within the family, and the laughter of a mother and child.* Gentleness and strength go hand in hand in making a peaceful and happy family.

Line 4
The fourth line is *one who is the light of the home.* All members of the home must reflect upon themselves and make sure that they are upholding the principles of the *Sage* for the common good.

Line 5
The fifth line is *one who is king of the home.* The one who upholds his principles is the one who will influence the family.

Line 6
The sixth line is *one who has put forth quality work.* If your thoughts and actions align in goodness, your family members will love you for it. The *Higher Power* will also guide your family to the right path.

38. K'uei - Opposition

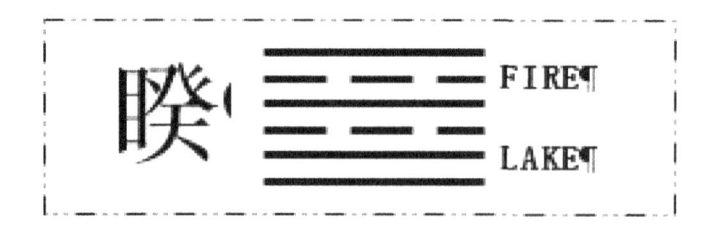

The representation

Judgment
Opposition is healthy when it is found in trivial matters. Opposition is necessary for progress and growth. Do not let it deter you or change your course of action if you believe in what you stand for. Rather, let it strengthen your convictions.

Image
Imagine the fire above the watery surface of a lake. The fire will never go underneath, just as the water cannot quench the flames. This is the image of Opposition. Do not let opposition sway your stance-remain firm in what you believe in, if what you believe in has proven to be correct and righteous.

Analysis

Some opposition comes from within. This opposition halts your progress and success, and only you can take away this obstacle. Remove all your negativity and focus on returning to the *Sage* so that you can become a better person. In the same way, when others block your path, hold steadfast in your principles, knowing that they are your salvation.

Line-by-line reading

Line 1

The first line is *a lost horse that will come back if not chased.* Do not manipulate a situation, but allow events to take their natural course. The horse will return if it is meant to.

Line 2
The second line is *one who meets his leader in an alley.* Reconciliation will come when you least expect it. Do not force yourself to meet formally with someone with whom you disagree; rather, let things run their course.

Line 3
The third line is *one who sees a wagon being dragged back.* While everything is against you now, accept your situation and improve yourself so that you can overcome it all.

Line 4
The fourth line is *one who opposes and causes his own isolation.* By succumbing to your negative inclinations, you have caused yourself to become abandoned and alone. Mend yourself and you will find the *Higher Power* ready to guide you

Line 5
The fifth line is *disappearing remorse.* Misunderstandings will mar your relationships with others. Do not let them take root in your heart, where they can no longer be removed.

Line 6
The sixth line is *one who opposes and causes his own isolation.* Do not isolate yourself out of fear-no harm will come to you from those you are afraid of.

39. Chien - Obstruction

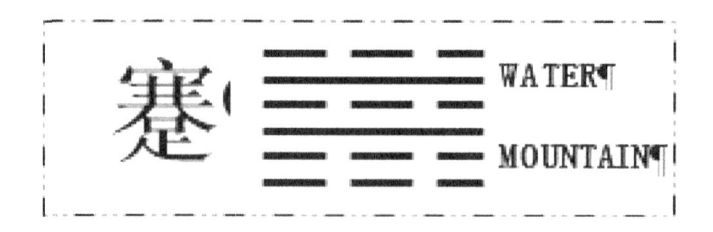

```
☵ WATER
☶ MOUNTAIN
```
塞

The representation

Judgment
Hardships *will* come and obstacles will present themselves, but perseverance will guide you through. First, though, a tactical retreat to a place of greater safety will allow you to gather allies.

Image
Imagine water flowing down from the mountaintops. This is the image of obstruction. Even if there are rocks and trees in its way, water will always reach the bottom. As such, remember that obstacles are there to make you stronger-to purify the water, so to speak.

Analysis

Imagine being in a deadly maze where each step you take leads to pain or demise. Your present situation may feel like that, like there is nowhere you *can* go because there are too many obstacles in the way. Do not let your negative emotions eat you up. In fact, the reason you are in this situation is *because* of your negative emotions and inclinations of jealousy, judgment, and desire. Look into yourself and examine your current state. Turn to the *Higher Power* for guidance and ask *Him* how you can make yourself better. Only when you correct yourself will your obstructions disappear.

Line-by-line reading

Line 1
Pushing through the obstructions will lead to your downfall. Take a step back to assess the situation, learn from your mistakes, and then slowly make progress.

Line 2
The second line is *a servant of the king who is bombarded with obstacles.* The situation you are in is no one's fault-what's done is done and blaming yourself or others will not get you anywhere. Rather, accept your situation and reflect upon yourself to start doing right.

Line 3
The third line is *one who meets with obstacles as he leaves, thus he returns.* The best course of action is retreat. Do not try to change the situation or power through anything. Retreat and correct your principles before returning. Do not give in to your ego.

Line 4
The fourth line is *one who meets with obstacles as he leaves, but who creates a united front as he returns.* Stay where you are and start gathering allies. Do not rush, but look to the *Sage* for guidance. When the time is right, you will find a clear path.

Line 5
The fifth line is *one whose friends come when the obstacles become overwhelming.* The most important thing right now is to realize that you will not prevail on your own. If you do not enlist help, then there is no hope of finding a clear path.

Line 6
The sixth line is *one who meets with obstacles as he leaves, but with good luck as he returns.* It is hard to get out of a slump, but it is harder still to help others out of a slump. As you improve yourself and find a clear path, help others who are in similar situations find their ways.

40. Hsieh - Deliverance

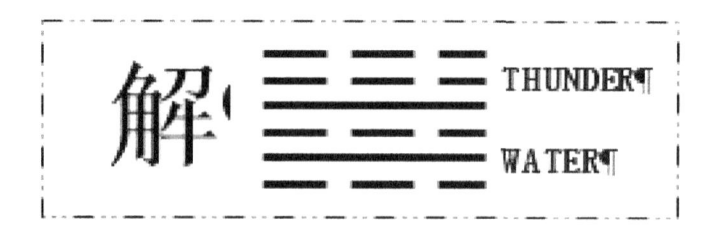

解 THUNDER
WATER

The representation

Judgment
Returning to your roots is the way to go if you have nowhere else to go. But if you have a goal, chase it now, as now is the time to chase your dreams while keeping the qualities of Deliverance in mind.

Image
Imagine the thunder and the rain settling over a town-and the people are not afraid. This is the image of deliverance. Forgive what has been done; hold no grudges.

Analysis

The obstructions and opposition that arose due to your negative inclinations are beginning to ease. To complete your deliverance, you must forgive others, restore and maintain your inner balance, and be patient. Your deliverance will come soon, so do not try to rush it or overdo it. Return to your correct path, and then stay wait- deliverance will soon follow.

Line-by-line reading

Line 1
Remain where are, and do not push yourself to move forward. You have triumphed over the obstacles. Remaining still will keep them from returning.

Line 2

The second line is *one who hunts down three foxes and is gifted a yellow arrow.* Now is the time to remove any remaining obstacles to your deliverance, but you must do so with proper intentions and actions. Feeding your ego by listening to it will lead you astray. Reflect upon yourself and turn away from your ego before you act.

Line 3
The third line is *one who can carry his burden and yet rides a carriage, thus inviting thieves.* If you are proud and try to put yourself on a pedestal above the rest, you will meet with misfortune. Humility is the key.

Line 4
The fourth line is *one who must not listen to the influence of his great toe.* You are beset by negative energy-from within yourself from the inferior people around you. Rid yourself of these negative influences so that progress may ensue.

Line 5
The fifth line is *one who is superior who can save himself.* You yourself must choose to get rid of the inferior elements in your life. Nothing will do it for you. Let go of what is holding you back so that you can move forward.

Line 6
The sixth line is *a prince who has shot down a hawk from a high wall.* Some negative influences can only be removed by force. Turn to the *Sage* for guidance and you will not go astray. Follow your ego and you will fail.

41. Sun - Decrease

損 ☶ MOUNTAIN
☱ LAKE

The representation

Judgment
When your wealth and power are on the wane, understand that this is a natural occurrence and do not try to hide from the fact. Adopt an attitude of modesty and simplicity as you adapt to your diminished circumstances, and use this time to reflect upon yourself and identify what needs to be changed. Sincerity will bring you farther.

Image
Imagine a lake at the foot of a mountain. This is the image of decrease. As a lake does not dream of climbing a mountain, man should restrain himself when it makes sense to practice restraint and instead direct his energies along the path to spiritual enlightenment.

Analysis

Everyone faces trials and tribulations. Now is a time of less-a decrease in the quality of life. Whatever you do, do not give in to your negative inclinations. It would be easy to give in to your ego and feel anger and despair, but do not let yourself fall. Rather, turn to the *Sage* for guidance, keeping a positive attitude and a correct outlook on life. Meditate and constantly improve yourself so that this time of drought will end.

Line-by-line reading

Line 1

The first line is *one who leaves as he has completed all his responsibilities.* Help others without expecting anything in return- even recognition. Meanwhile, only accept help from those who can afford to give it.

Line 2
The second line is *one who perseveres.* Persevere in your own principles and maintain your dignity. It does you good to remain true to your values as you endeavor to help others.

Line 3
The third line states *one who travels with companions will find himself alone, but one who travels alone will find new companions.* Remove those who will influence you negatively to make room for better companions. The *Sage* will guide you.

Line 4
The fourth line is *one who endeavors to improve himself.* Improving yourself is the first step to calling others to you. They will help you when the time comes that you need it.

Line 5
The fifth line is *one who has someone to support him.* Maintain innocence within yourself and you will not be led astray; your path to success is sure.

Line 6
The sixth line is *one who improves himself without disadvantaging others.* Generosity and helpfulness in times of trouble will start your path to the *increase.* Do not let despair and selfishness cloud your judgment; rather, keep giving and it will return to you.

42. I - Increase

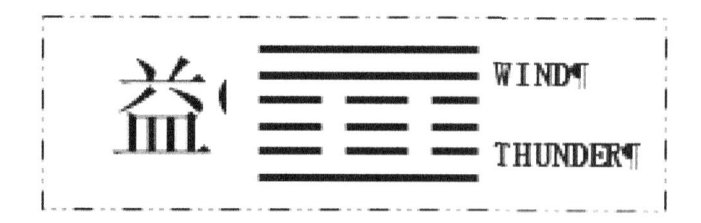

益 WIND
    THUNDER

The representation

Judgment
As the name suggests, now is the time to act. Increase yourself in areas where you need to improve. If you are planning something big, act now, while keeping your principles in mind.

Image
Imagine wind working with the thunders. This is the image of increase. Do whatever is good and shun whatever is bad-for yourself and others.

Analysis

You are experiencing a time of plenty-a time of increase. But do not get comfortable, for as bad times always come to an end, so do the good. Instead of simply enjoying the ride, make the most of your present opportunities and prepare yourself for the future. Improve yourself and help those around you, and you will find that even when times of trouble return, you will not want for anything.

Line-by-line reading

Line 1
The first line is *one who has achieved greatness.* You have been given a golden opportunity, and you must not waste it. Outdo yourself in effort, and help others with what you have gained.

Line 2
The second line is *one who has someone to support him.* Stay true to your principles and to the *Higher Power* and you will achieve your goals with *His* help. Nothing will stand in your way.

Line 3
The third line is *one who profits from adversity.* Meet hard times with innocence and the correct attitude and you will not only get through them but come out ahead.

Line 4
The fourth line is *one who stands on neutral ground.* Continue helping others, acting as a peacemaker when need be. Follow the example set by the *Sage* and you will prosper.

Line 5
The fifth line is *one who is kindhearted.* Help others because it is the right thing to do, not because you want to gain thereby. Virtue is its own reward.

Line 6
The sixth line is *one who does not improve his companions.* You need the help of others to further yourself. Thus, help those below you so that you build the proper foundation.

43. Kuai - Breakthrough (Resoluteness)

夬 LAKE
    HEAVEN

The representation

Judgment
Now is the time to fight for what is right so that evil may be decisively overcome-but do not do so in a violent manner, as this will only engender more strife. Stand firm in your ideals and look forward to achieving a breakthrough in whatever standstill you have been experiencing.

Image
Imagine the lake rising *above* the heavens. It seems impossible, yet the lake was able to make a breakthrough. So will you. Remain persevering and patient, and you will achieve your goal. Then, as rain eventually falls to the earth, you may share your gains with others.

Analysis

You are about to overcome a great difficulty, but you must handle this situation with the right attitude. A breakthrough-whether against your own flaws or some external force-is coming. Make sure you are standing by your principles and working for a positive outcome. But beware that overcoming challenges *can* lead to inflated pride. Do not let your pride overcome you, else you will fail. Rather, continually look within yourself and uphold what is right so that your breakthrough will matter and the obstacle you overcame will not return.

Line-by-line reading

Line 1
The first line is *forward striding toes.* Move forward, but at a measured pace. Overreaching yourself because of your ego will only bring despair.

Line 2
The second line is *a sudden cry for help.* Prepare yourself for danger, as it will come unexpectedly.

Line 3
The third line is *the power found in the cheekbones.* Your ego tells you that you need to act now, but you know there is something wrong. Do not act until you see a clear path.

Line 4
The fourth line is *one who has a hard time walking for his thighs are skinless.* Do not try to force change upon your current state when you know in your heart that it is impossible. Rather, stay still and quiet yourself, turning to the *Sage* for guidance.

Line 5
The fifth line is *one who removes weeds with a firm resolution.* Remove the inferior elements surrounding yourself and proceed only in what is right and just.

Line 6
The sixth line is *no one sounded the alarm.* You may not know when you are falling back into despair, so keep your wits about you. Your attitude in handling these situations matters more than you realize.

44. Kou - Coming to Meet

姤 ▬▬▬▬ HEAVEN
▬▬▬▬
▬▬▬▬
▬▬▬▬ WIND
▬▬▬▬
▬▬ ▬▬

The representation

Judgment
Meeting with others who have the same ideals as you will bring good fortune. But do not entangle yourself with foolhardy persons who have no values.

Image
Imagine the winds billowing under the heavens, the winds that bring things together. This is the image of Coming to Meet. Let your voice be heard, your plans be known.

Analysis

Darkness and inferiority are coming to tempt you. You will be swayed to act by your ego, your despair, or even your false confidence if you give in to this sudden wave of darkness. Rather, retreat within yourself and fortify your walls. Do not let the influence of your inferiors affect you. Remain balanced and upright, and you will make it through.

Line-by-line reading

Line 1
The first line is *one uses a brake of bronze to check himself.* Remain balanced; do not let your negative inclinations take the wheel.

Line 2

The second line is *one with fish in his tank.* Do not answer darkness with violence. Merely contain it, retreat within yourself and maintain your upright nature.

Line 3
The third line is *one who has a hard time walking for his thighs are skinless.* While moving forward may seem like an attractive course of action, remember that there are good reasons not to. Prepare yourself, but do not act.

Line 4
The fourth line is *one who has a tank but without the fish.* Gentleness will get you through the hard times. Others will tempt you to get mad and lash out, but you must remain tolerant and gentle to maintain valuable relationships. These two qualities will pull you through.

Line 5
The fifth line is *willow leaves shading a melon.* Use your actions to cause change. Set an example of how others must act and they will follow suit. Do not berate, lead.

Line 6
The sixth line is *one who uses his horns to accept new things.* Meditate on the *Higher Power,* for this is the answer to your troubles. Do not let inferior inclinations influence your course of action, whether they stem from others or yourself.

45. Ts'ui - Gathering Together (Massing)

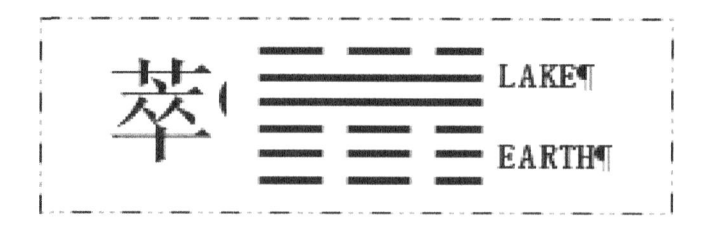

萃 — LAKE / EARTH

The representation

Judgment
If you have been planning something, now is the time to act, with the help of others. Gather together, for strength can be found in numbers.

Image
Imagine the earth underneath a lake, with all the elements coming together. This is the image of Gathering Together. Prepare yourself for what you would least expect-do not become ignorant.

Analysis

There is strength in numbers, so to speak. Work with those you trust, those who will not influence you negatively, and those who will admonish you when you need it. Remember, while you are in a group, you also need to improve yourself. Do not forget to reflect upon your attitudes so that you can properly become a member of the group. If you present a good attitude, as the *I Ching* teaches you, you will influence others to do good as well. Gather together with others who are like you, and you will all achieve your goals.

Line-by-line reading

Line 1
The first line is *one who starts out sincere, but does not push through with his sincerity.* Hesitating to do right will lead to your

downfall. Continue with sincerity to achieve your goals, and do not be afraid to ask for help if you need it.

Line 2
The second line is *one who lets himself be led.* Be attuned to the callings of the *Higher Power* and follow *Him* while leading others in the correct path.

Line 3
The third line is *one who pushes for unity amidst sighs.* While may not be accepted immediately, do not withdraw from the group. Remain true to your principles and you will be rewarded. Do not let humiliation cloud your judgment.

Line 4
Remain unselfish and you will meet with good fortune.

Line 5
The fifth line is *one who unites and leads his subjects.* Remember that your associates must be inherently good; otherwise, they will corrupt the rest. You must set a good example and improve yourself to improve those around you.

Line 6
The sixth line is *one who sighs and weeps.* If your attempts at fellowship are rebuffed, following the *Higher Power* is the only possible course of action. Do so, and your failure will turn to success.

46. Shêng - Pushing Upward

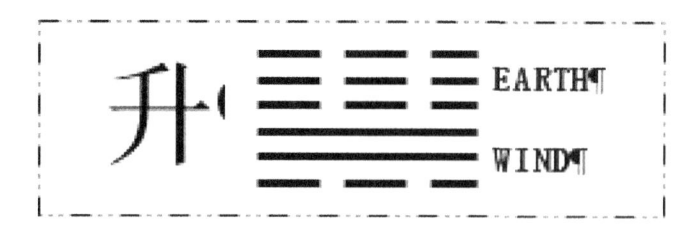

升 ☷ EARTH
   ☴ WIND

The representation

Judgment
Pushing upward is striving to become better-in character and practice. Remain vigilant and keep improving so that you will meet with success.

Image
Imagine the wood growing from within the earth, surrounded by darkness, yet still persevering. This is the image of Pushing Upward. Keep pushing, with advances both strong and weak, towards progress.

Analysis

Now is a time of plenty, as long as you work for it. You will meet with success if only you remain humble and kind-hearted. While you are successful, do not let pride take over, and make sure that you continually reflect upon yourself so that you are not overtaken by inferior elements. Put your trust in the *Higher Power* and believe that you will not be led astray. Do not let fear or doubt cloud your judgment, either. Stay true to your principles and you will be fine.

Line-by-line reading

Line 1
The first line is *one who advances with confidence.* Do not be egotistical, but realize that you have what it takes to make things

happen with the help of the *Higher Power*

Line 2
The second line is *one with sincerity.* Be yourself, even when you feel inadequate or out of place, and you will be fine. Sincerity and humility are the keys to your success.

Line 3
The third line is *one who perseveres in advancing into an empty city.* There are no more obstacles between you and success, but your relationship with the *Sage* will determine whether or not you truly attain that success.

Line 4
The fourth line is *one who receives his place on Mount Ch'i.* Success will come to those who look within themselves and continuously seek improvement through diligent effort.

Line 5
The fifth line is *one who perseveres.* Principled and neutral perseverance will benefit you. Slow and steady wins the race.

Line 6
The sixth line is *one who perseveres into the darkness.* If you let ego and ambition lead you blindly, you *will* fail.

47. K'un - Oppression (Exhaustion)

The representation

Judgment
People will not believe you-that is Oppression. But like all obstacles, it can be overcome. Do not let oppression get in the way of your success. Stand firm in your beliefs, no matter what others say.

Image
Imagine a lake without water-a dried up patch of ground. This is the image of exhaustion. Do not let exhaustion make you sway your path. Instead, remain persevering in all that you do, and accept that the road will be difficult.

Analysis

A time of trouble is upon you once again. Remain confident in your principles and you will be fine. If you feel despair or sadness, then it is likely that you are harboring negative emotions and detrimental goals. Remember, reflect upon yourself and you will find the right path. Oppression can be overcome with the help of the *Sage* if you remain upright and thoughtful.

Line-by-line reading

Line 1
The first line is *one who sits under a tree against his will.* Do not despair; rather, accept the situation and look at it in a positive light. Remain happy and cheerful, and you will overcome anything.

Line 2
The second line is *one who eating and drinking in an oppressed state.* Exhaustion is close at hand. But if you feel this exhaustion, then you are doing something wrong. Ask the *Sage* for guidance and *He* will guide you to healing.

Line 3
The third line is *one who has allowed himself to be restricted by stones, and who is willingly leaning on thorns.* Retreating is the best course of action in this situation. If you keep pushing at a thorny wall, it will not move and you will only hurt yourself.

Line 4
The fourth line is *one who is oppressed while riding in a golden carriage.* Do not be discouraged if your efforts are thwarted. While it may seem humiliating, trust in the *Higher Power* and you will eventually succeed.

Line 5
The fifth line is *one whose nose and feet have been removed.* Remain humble and honest, and you will power through. Oppression ends; just wait for it to happen while quietly communing with the *Sage*.

Line 6
The sixth line is *one who is restrained with vines or standing on a high ledge, telling himself "movement will bring regret."* If you seek to advance, you must believe that you can do so. Do not give in to despair. Rather, seek help to overcome obstacles and oppression.

48. Ching - the Well

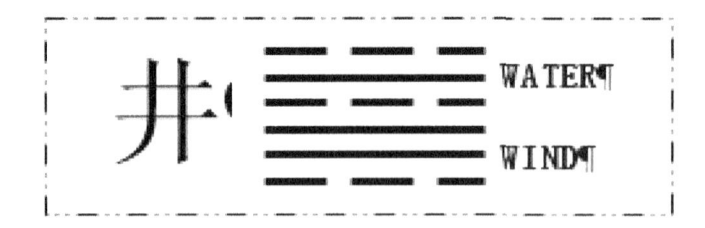

井 ䷯ WATER / WIND

The representation

Judgment
The well stands for permanence. While others may be changing, the well will never change. If you can successfully draw water from it, you will meet with good fortune. If the ropes snap or the bucket breaks, you must look within yourself and figure out what caused it.

Image
Imagine water over wood. This is the image of a well-simple yet functional. People meet at the watering hole all the time, and a good man will encourage everyone to work together.

Analysis

There are two kinds of well-an external well and your internal well. The *I Ching* can nourish both, as it contains spiritual wisdom as well as sound advice on how you should act in times of trouble. Historically, all communities needed a well to survive. In the same way, you cannot survive without feeding your internal and external wells. If anything you are planning may cloud your internal or external well, then you need to change plans. Do not do anything that may add mud to the clean water.

Line-by-line reading

Line 1

The first line is *an old well whose waters have become mud.* If you leave your principles behind, you will destroy your inner well. It will not end well for you.

Line 2
The second line is *a well or basket with a hole through which the water escapes.* The waters of the well will be inaccessible to you until you turn to your better nature. You cannot draw water with a broken basket.

Line 3
The third line is *a clean well which no one uses.* You *know* what is right from wrong, and yet you do not heed your own sound advice and good judgment. Turn to the *Higher Power* to guide you to using your internal and external wells properly.

Line 4
The fourth line is *lining a well.* You must line the well properly by looking within yourself and working on your own attitude. Only when the well has been properly lined can you move forward with your next course of action.

Line 5
The fifth line is *a well containing clear waters from a spring, one that everyone can use.* You have the ability to draw water from the well. But just drawing the water is not enough for nourishment. You must drink the water for the nourishment to enter you.

Line 6
The sixth line is *one who uses a well without hesitation and encounters no obstacles.* Wealth is not riches, but the ability to choose what is right over wrong. When you have achieved a clean internal and external well that you *use* and *cherish*, then you will progress and effect progress for those around you as well.

49. Ko - Revolution (Molting)

```
革    ═══ ═══  LAKE
      ═══════
      ═══════
      ═══════
      ═══════  FIRE
      ═══ ═══
```

The representation

Judgment
People will listen to you because you speak truth and goodness. Starting a revolution now will lead to success. Change is imminent, and you must become the catalyst, keeping both sincerity and perseverance in your heart.

Image
Imagine a fire inside a lake. While the waters will strangle it, the fire continues to burn. This is the image of revolution. Do not let the waters put out your fire.

Analysis

Hold on to your principles, for a change is coming and you need to have the right attitude to get through it. If you seek change, then you need to meditate and look within yourself to see if you are truly ready for this kind of change. You must be spurred by positive emotions and inclinations, not your pride or selfishness. In the same way, if you want change on the outside, then you must first enact an inner revolution of sorts. Cleanse yourself and what you perceive to be wrong about your path. Only when you have changed your inner self can you start working on changing the outside, and then those around you.

Line-by-line reading

Line 1
The first line is *one bound in the yellow hide of a cow.* If you move prematurely or unnecessarily, you will only cause more trouble. Stay still and wait for change to come with the right attitude of humility and patience. A clear, safe path will present itself when the time is right.

Line 2
The second line *subjects who are rebelling against the crown, for change.* It is time to act, but turn to your humility, not your ego, for guidance in your next steps. Make sure that your foundation is secure before you start your revolution.

Line 3
The third line is *one who starts the revolution neither too soon nor too late.* Hesitation and hastiness will both be your downfall. Do not let a miscalculation ruin your revolution.

Line 4
The fourth line is *disappearing remorse.* Remain blameless and your revolution will prosper. Let yourself be run by your negative inclinations, and you will fail.

Line 5
The fifth line is *one who has the support of many because he has heeded the Higher Power.* Align yourself with the cries of the many, for their cries are what the world needs. If you start a revolution founded on the needs of those who have nothing, many will follow you.

Line 6
The sixth line is *one who appreciates all progress, even the smallest.* Turn to the *Sage* for guidance and advice, and he will lead you to the proper path. After great change, take small steps; slow progress is still progress.

50. Ting - the Caldron

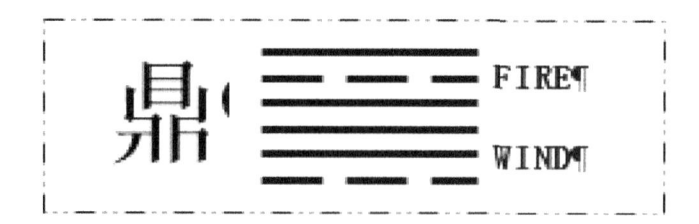

鼎　══　FIRE
　　═══
　　══　WIND
　　═══
　　═══

The representation

Judgment
The caldron signifies supreme good fortune. If you have cast this oracle, then it is time to act so long as you keep goodness in your heart.

Image
Imagine fire over wood. This is the image of the caldron. Follow the right path, and you will be guided to success.

Analysis

The caldron symbolizes the nourishment you derive from your soul and spirit. If you remain true to your principles, then it remains full. Your spirit is pure and the *Higher Power* will be able to help and guide you as much as you need. If the opposite is true, then you will have difficulty advancing. Contemplate and consecrate yourself to the *Sage*, and all will be well.

Line-by-line reading

Line 1
The first line is *an inverted caldron.* Turn the caldron over and pour out all your iniquities. Through ridding yourself of iniquities, you open yourself to more possibilities.

Line 2

The second line is *a caldron with food.* Seek nourishment from the *Sage* and not others. Do not let the negative inclinations of others resound with your own-do not let them influence you to change from light to dark.

Line 3
The third line is *a caldron with a changed handle.* While others may not recognize your virtues, you are still the same person. If you act with the right motivations, then people will eventually listen.

Line 4
The fourth line is *a caldron with broken legs.* You are a leader now, but if you let your negative inclinations run the show, then you will fail and ultimately experience humiliation and defeat.

Line 5
The fifth line is *a caldron with golden handles.* People will help you if they see that you are both just and kind. Turn away from your negative inclinations, and you will find yourself with many supporters.

Line 6
The sixth line is *a caldron embedded with a piece of jade.* Stay close to the *Sage,* for his counsel is invaluable. Bring that counsel to those around you so that they too may share in your blessings.

51. Chen - the Arousing (Shock, Thunder)

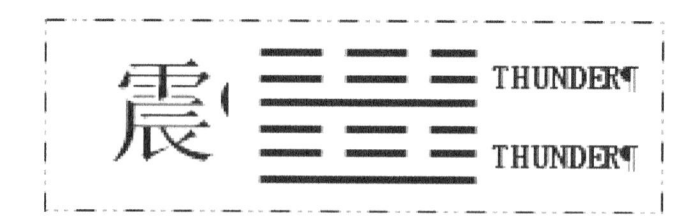

The representation

Judgment
Be ready for surprises, as life will often throw them your way. Do not let surprises frighten you, for they will bring success.

Image
Imagine hearing repeated thunder, getting louder and louder. This is the image of the arousing. It means something is about to happen, and you must be prepared to go along for the ride.

Analysis

If you cast this hexagram, then you are about to be reminded that life is unpredictable-as such, shocking events will come and go. But you need not react to each and every one of them. In this case, you need to step back, analyze the event, and then turn to the *Higher Power* for guidance. Learn from the shock and open your mind to a world of possibilities. This symbolizes a new beginning, an opportunity to learn that you should not miss.

Line-by-line reading

Line 1
The first line is *one who gets shocked and laughs.* While something shocking will immediately be construed as bad, if you step back and look again, you will find that it teaches you something. You will be happy to have learned something.

Line 2
The second line is *one who is endangered because of his surprise.* Do not let your surprise spur you into action. Rather, contemplate what has happened and what the best course of action is next.

Line 3
The third line is *one who is distraught because of shock.* While shocking events may leave you confused, you *should not* let them run your life. Use them to find new ways of action, and you will be fine.

Line 4
The fourth line is *one whose sudden, shocked movements make him sink into mud.* Stop resisting your situation. While it came without warning, life sometimes does that. Rather, accept your current situation and wait until a clear path out presents itself. Learn rather than struggle.

Line 5
The fifth line is *one who is surrounded by shocking situations, causing trouble-but does not give in to complete despair.* Remain balanced and contemplative, and you will be fine. The shocking situations *cannot* harm you if you do not let them.

Line 6
The sixth line is *one who is caught unawares and is paralyzed by shock.* Following a shock, you may need some time to process what has happened. Do not act too soon, even if others are urging you to do so. Take your time, remain balanced and you will be fine.

52. Kên - Keeping Still, Mountain

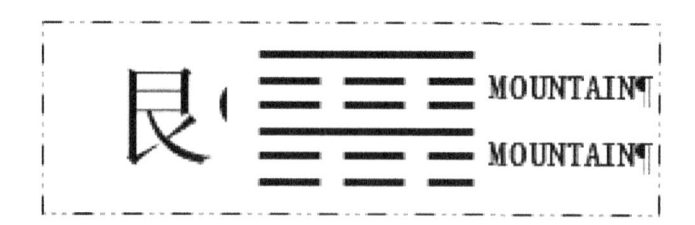

The representation

Judgment
Keep still, contemplating your thoughts and actions. Do not let others influence your judgment if you know you are on the righteous path.

Image
Imagine the mountains, standing tall and never bending or succumbing to the wind. This is the image of keeping still. Keep still and stay upright. Do not let others cloud your thoughts, nor let bad decisions ruin your life. You know which path is correct, so choose the right path.

Analysis

You are experiencing turmoil because you are listening to your emotions too much. Calm down, take a deep breath, a step back, then ponder. What you need right now is to isolate yourself and meditate on your emotions as they come and go. Observe what you are feeling. Do not resist feeling the way you feel-you will get nowhere. But do not act on your feelings. When you have identified which emotions are causing you the most trouble, turn to the *Higher Power* for assistance on what you must do with them.

Line-by-line reading

Line 1

The first line is *one who keeps his toes at rest.* Like a mountain, stay still in innocence and rest. You will find your way back to the path as soon as is necessary.

Line 2
The second line is *one who keeps his calves at rest.* You may want to move, but keep yourself at rest. Do not let others spur you into premature action.

Line 3
The third line is *one who keeps his hips at rest.* While at this time it may *seem* necessary to force yourself to keep still, this is not a good course of action. Forcing something that should come naturally will lead to your demise.

Line 4
The fourth line is *one who keeps his trunk at rest.* Accept your situation and still your heart. If you become troubled, turn to the *Sage* for guidance.

Line 5
The fifth line is *one who keeps his jaw still.* While you may feel restlessness starting to take root, do not speak brashly. Stay peaceful and you will find happiness.

Line 6
The sixth line is *one who keeps his noble-hearted self still.* Remain still and accept all things as they are, as this is the only thing you can do to remain on the right path. In the end, you will be at peace.

53. Chien - Development (Gradual Progress)

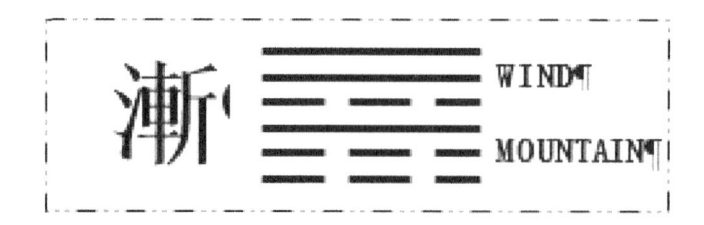

渐 ▆▆▆ WIND
    ▆ ▆
    ▆▆▆
    ▆▆▆ MOUNTAIN
    ▆ ▆
    ▆ ▆

The representation

Judgment
The start of development signifies good fortune if development is done for the right cause. Remember that the new can make things change for the better, and that in any new endeavor it is best to proceed slowly and correctly.

Image
Imagine a lone tree sprouting on top a mountain. This is the image of development. Just as the tree takes years to grow but signifies the beginning of a new spring and bountiful harvest, you must remain firm in your principles over time to become the catalyst for progress.

Analysis

Today, people want everything to go fast. And by fast, they mean *super*-fast. The problem with fast development is that foundations are often not built correctly. Rather than lay a good foundation, people will jump right in the middle and then lose everything they built in the blink of an eye. The *I Ching* advises that now is a time for patience and building foundations. Do not jump into something without first preparing the roots and making sure they hold fast to the ground.

Line-by-line reading

Line 1
The first line is *a wild goose slowly waddling to the shore.* You are starting on your journey, albeit slowly. Do not let doubts and fears cloud your judgment and make you turn around.

Line 2
The second line is *a wild goose slowly waddling toward a cliff.* When you reach a place of greater security, you must remember to share your good fortune with others.

Line 3
The third line is *a wild goose slowly waddling toward a plateau.* Do not attempt to advance in unsuitable ways merely for the sake of progress. Remain balanced until you can find an answer to your problems within yourself or with others.

Line 4
The fourth line is *a wild goose slowly waddling toward a tree.* Make the most of whatever situation you find yourself in, for that is the only thing you can do. Do not resist, and good things will come to you.

Line 5
The fifth line is *a wild goose slowly waddling toward the summit.* While your achievements will benefit you, others will not understand-they may even go so far as to criticize you for your course of action. Do not let them sway you.

Line 6
The sixth line is *a wild goose slowly waddling toward the clouds.* If you hold still and stay true to the principles of the *Sage,* you will find yourself at the top of the world. Remain humble, but influence people to follow in your path towards the *Sage*.

54. Kuei Mei - the Marrying Maiden

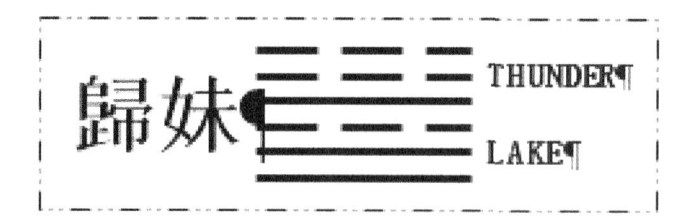

歸妹 ☳ THUNDER
       ☱ LAKE

The representation

Judgment
The marrying maiden reminds us that our relationships are important, and that they must be taken care of. As lies and selfishness can break a relationship, so can misplaced desires and imbalance. Work on your relationships before undertaking anything of importance.

Image
Imagine thunder booming over a lake. This is the image of the marrying maiden. If you do not maintain your relationships, they will lead to your detriment.

Analysis

This hexagram means that you need to focus on your relationships. When you enter a relationship, desire often comes into the picture. You desire more from your partner, from your friend, from your brother or sister. And when these desires are not satisfied, or when conflicts arise, it is easy for you to abandon the relationships altogether. The *I Ching* states that nothing can be rushed in a relationship, and that desires will only lead to demise. Rather, both acceptance and careful planning are needed. You must accept that sometimes things will be hard, but if you work on your relationship, things will get better. In the same way, if you rush into getting into, getting out of, or amending a relationship, you will get hurt. Again, relationships must not be rushed; they must be cultivated and cared for.

Line-by-line reading

Line 1
The first line is *a younger sister becoming a concubine.* While your role is small, you still have a role. Hone yourself and practice staying true to your principles until the time comes when your role is more significant.

Line 2
The second line is *one who has one eye but can still see.* Keep looking for the good in those who surround you, because that will be your salvation. Things may look bleak now, but they will right themselves in time.

Line 3
The third line is *a younger sister who marries into slavery.* Fate is cruel, but sometimes we must accept that and make the best of things. Do not let your ego and selfishness spur your actions.

Line 4
The fourth line is *a younger sister who delays her marriage.* Patience is definitely a virtue. Do not rush into things, and the right paths will present themselves.

Line 5
The fifth line is *the humble attire of those in attendance of the wedding ceremony.* When things do not go as you had hoped, the best course of action is to accept this and adapt to the changed circumstances. If you remain steadfast, you will achieve success.

Line 6
The sixth line is *a woman who carries a fruit basket with no fruits.* Even if you do the right things, if you do them for the wrong reasons,

you are still doing wrong. Follow the *Higher Power* and heed *His* guidance.

55. Fêng - Abundance (Fullness)

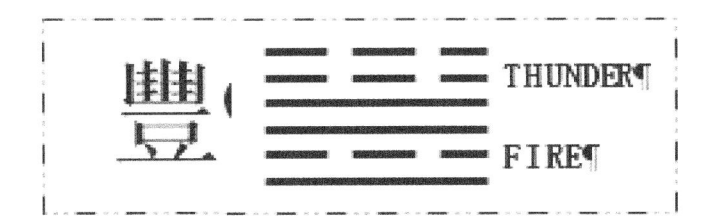

```
☳ THUNDER
☲ FIRE
```

The representation

Judgment
Be content in your abundance, and do not ask for more. Rather, stay humble and helpful, helping your neighbors when they need it. Now is a time of success; prepare yourself and do not waste it.

Image
Imagine thunder and lightning filling the heavens in a display of power. This is the image of Abundance. A powerful time is upon us, and you must make the best of it and enjoy it while it lasts.

Analysis

Thunder and lightning filling the heavens strikes fear into the hearts of those who see-it is powerful, but only for a few seconds. In the same way, when a moment of pure abundance comes, it will only last for a moment-seize it. Always return to observation and counsel from the *Higher Power*. Your influence on others will sometimes reach a peak. And when that peak comes, make use of it in the *right* way. When it leaves, do not cling to your influence. Rather, let it go and watch for its return.

Line-by-line reading

Line 1
The first line is *one who meets with leaders and becomes one himself.* Union is possible if everyone has the same goals and

ideals. Work together as much as you can while abundance is available. Let go willingly when the abundance ends.

Line 2
The second line is *closed curtains at noon.* Follow the truth and the light to the best possible outcome. If you wallow in the darkness of distrust and doubt, you will miss opportunities.

Line 3
The third line is *a bushes that blot out the sun.* Sometimes a host of seemingly minor obstructions together become so overwhelming as to block progress altogether. Remember that this is not your fault, and that the path of the *Higher Power* can never be closed off forever.

Line 4
The fourth line is *closed curtains at noon.* Remain modest, heed the advice of the worthy, and do not succumb to the darkness.

Line 5
The fifth line is *blessing and fame nearing.* Even with all your achievements, remember to remain humble; much of your success is due to the help and advice of others. Humility will allow the *Sage* to bless you and guide you more.

Line 6
The sixth line is *a rich man who does not see others.* If you let your pride and selfishness get in the way, your abundance will end. Give to those who need help and stay in the light of the *Sage*.

56. Lu - the Wanderer

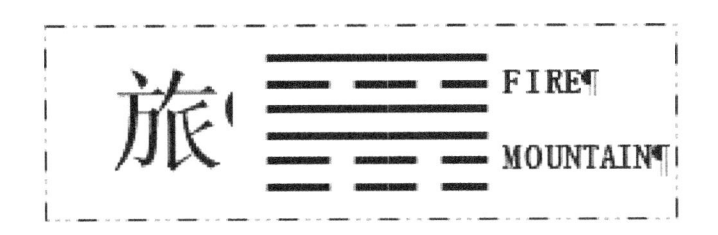

旅 ☲ FIRE
   ☶ MOUNTAIN

The representation

Judgment
Perseverance will bring you success, and small, careful actions will lead to progress. While you do not yet know where your final destination is, the *Higher Power* will guide you.

Image
Imagine fire on the top of a mountain, deciding which way to go as the wind guides it. This is the image of the wanderer. Stay clear-minded in your travels and proceed with both alacrity and caution.

Analysis

The world remains wide and strange for each and every one of us. The earth is our temporary home, and while we are here, we must proceed- but we must proceed with caution. The *I Ching* reminds us that you need to careful while wandering. Make sure your friends are true and that you remain humble and persevering. All these will come back to you in the end. While you are in this land, help all whom you can help and become an example for others who may look to you for guidance. Do not seek conflict, and do not encourage it. Rather, act as a wanderer does and keep to yourself-careful curiosity and glee aside.

Line-by-line reading

Line 1

The first line is *the wanderer who is occupied with meaningless things.* If you waste time on trivial things, you will lose your way. Maintain your seriousness of purpose, and bring only what you need to stay on the right path.

Line 2
The second line is *the wanderer who stays at an inn with all of his things.* If you have remained humble and kind all your life, you will win friends to help you when the journey gets tiring.

Line 3
The third line is *the wanderer whose inn burns down.* If you let your ego and misplaced curiosity guide your actions, you will lose your resting place. Return to your original principles and you will be fine.

Line 4
The fourth line is *the wanderer who rests in a shelter with his livelihood and axe.* Even when your position seems tenable, you cannot rest easy. When you need help, no one will answer your call, and you must be prepared to defend yourself by yourself.

Line 5
The fifth line is *the wanderer shooting a pheasant.* When you find a way to prove yourself worthy, you will meet with success.

Line 6
The sixth line is *a burning bird's nest.* If you become overconfident and are careless in your travels, you will meet with failure.

57. Sun - the Gentle (the Penetrating, Wind)

The representation

Judgment
Have a goal in mind and you will not stray. Small steps toward your goal will lead you to success. Keep gentleness in your heart, especially in times of trouble, and do not be too proud to seek help.

Image
Imagine the winds billowing through grass, one gust after the other. This is the image of gentleness. Spread your wishes as the wind does and others will follow.

Analysis

When you are faced with a problem, the most energetic course of action is often the most foolhardy one. The *I Ching* advises that you ponder your problem before acting. You should first create a clear goal and keep that goal in mind. If you just eliminate the problem in the fastest way possible, you will only be achieving a temporary solution. Second, you need to look within yourself and use the gently penetrating principles upon yourself. Is there anything that you need to change? Lastly, do not let your negative inclinations guide you. No matter what, you should not try to manipulate the situation. Hand it over to the *Sage* and *He* will make sure that everything will be fine.

Line-by-line reading

Line 1

The first line is *one who is in advance and retreat.* Look at the bigger picture to see whether the smart move is to advance or retreat. Then choose one-and stick with your choice. If you can advance with safety, take steps forward. If you cannot, retreat willingly.

Line 2
The second line is *penetrating beneath the bed.* Some hidden evil is trying to sway your good nature. Do not let hidden influences, from either within or without, change your principles.

Line 3
The third line is *repeated, violent penetration.* Make necessary corrections to your attitude when you find that you are in a slump, but then let the matter be. Repeatedly second-guessing yourself will do you no good..

Line 4
The fourth line is *vanishing remorse.* Make sure that you are clean within and without, and then proceed surely. Cleanse yourself of negative inclinations and things will right themselves before you realize it.

Line 5
The fifth line is *vanishing remorse and perseverance.* When contemplating a change of course, hold on to the principles that the *Sage* has taught you and you will find success. Remove from yourself negative emotions and desires and you will find the right path.

Line 6
The sixth line is *penetrating beneath the bed.* If you are too weak to fight your external opposition, it does not profit you to seek it out. Instead, look to yourself and improve yourself. Just because you know who is harming you does not mean that there is anything you can do about it.

58. Tui - the Joyous, Lake

The representation

Judgment
Persevering joy will lead you to success.

Image
Imagine two lakes resting one on top of the other, their inhabitants mingling with their new neighbors. This is the image of the Joyous. Turn to your friends when you feel lost.

Analysis

If you want lasting joy, then you need both patience and principles. No matter what happens, you cannot steal joy from others or force joy upon yourself; you need to cultivate it and let it blossom. The *I Ching* reminds us to stay away from the desires of the world, for that is not true joy. In the same way, it also advises us to stay away from the shortcuts that may lead to our detriment.

Line-by-line reading

Line 1
The first line is *inward harmony and joyfulness.* Be content with what you have, and joy will follow. Do not desire worldly things, for they will not bring you true joy.

Line 2
The second line is *joyfulness from sincerity.* Worldly pleasures do not last. In seeking joyfulness, make sure you remain sincere and

principled, or else you will find something resembling joy that is actually fleeting and harmful.

Line 3
The third line is *one who takes joy indiscriminately.* Even if you do not seek them out, it is not a good practice to find joy in worldly things. Even in peaceful times, guard yourself against these negative inclinations.

Line 4
The fourth line is *one who is restlessly seeking joy.* The *Higher Power* can help you attain true joy, but only if you first stop searching for it in a world that can only give you temporary happiness.

Line 5
The fifth line is *one who trusts in another who can hurt him.* Innocence and truth are the most important things when searching for true joy. Do not rely on people who will tell you otherwise or influence you negatively.

Line 6
The sixth line is *one who is susceptible to temptation.* The *I Ching* advises detachment from the world as the best course of action when searching for happiness. Stay grounded in your principles and you will be fine.

59. Huan - Dispersion (Dissolution)

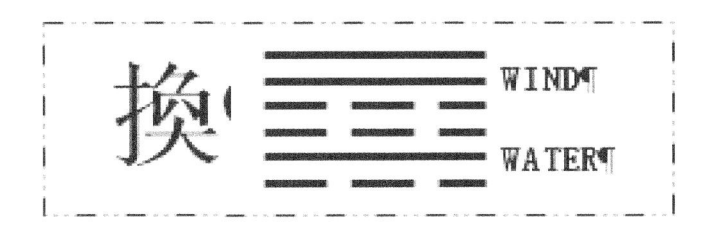

换 ☴ WIND
☵ WATER

The representation

Judgment
Your values are still your top priority. Dispersing selfishness and bad attitudes with gentleness and resolve will greatly benefit you.

Image
Imagine the wind blowing over the waters, blending everything together without barriers. This is the image of dispersion. Hold your principles near and get rid of thoughts that do not benefit you.

Analysis

Let the warm winds blow over you and remove the barriers between yourself and others. Holding on to negative emotions and inclinations toward isolation and selfishness will keep you from progressing. The *I Ching* is reminding you now that it is time to stop being standoffish. Become more kind and gentle, and remove your inflexibility and harshness. Let dispersion take its course and join you in unity with your fellowmen.

Line-by-line reading

Line 1
The first line is *one who rescues with a strong horse.* Strive towards truthfulness and understanding and you will find help. Do not let conflict strive in your encampment.

Line 2

The second line is *the disappearing remorse of one who finds support within himself.* Do not rebuke others when you have problems. Rather, adjust your attitude and allow yourself to see the best in others.

Line 3
The third line is *one who cares not for his own well-being.* Put aside your desires, ambition, and other negative inclinations. Put the needs of others first, and then you will find your own success.

Line 4
The fourth line is *one who disbands his clique.* Willingly remove from your life the people who are holding you back or negatively influencing you. Return to them only when you are strong enough to shun their influence and influence them in return.

Line 5
The fifth line is *one whose cries disappear like sweat.* Create understanding in a group by showing them a singular, moral goal. This way, all conflict will be dispersed.

Line 6
The sixth line is *one who discards bloody wounds and fears.* Avoiding danger to yourself and your loved ones is not cowardice but a noble act. Remove negative emotions such as fear and worry, and you will be guided by the *Sage*.

60. Chieh - Limitation

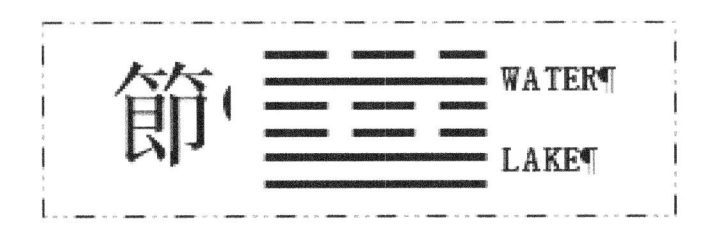

節 — WATER / LAKE

The representation

Judgment
Limit yourself when it is necessary. Know when to hold back, and you will meet with success.

Image
Imagine the water over the lakes. It does not exceed its bounds, nor does it overflow to the villages. This is the image of proper limitations. Limit yourself where limits need to be placed so that you will remain upright and virtuous.

Analysis

If you want to live correctly, you need to set limits upon yourself- rules, of sorts. But remember that you cannot emplace too many rules or else you will suffocate. Set your goals, responsibilities, self-needs, and requirements, and set them in stone. Change them only if you think they are no longer applicable. If you live by certain limits, then you will improve and grow. If you live life without limits, chaos will ensue. Limit yourself with the guidance of the *Sage,* and you will succeed.

Line-by-line reading

Line 1
The first line is *one who does not leave the courtyard through the outer door.* If you respect your limits and remain true to the *Higher*

Power, then help will come when you need it most.

Line 2
The second line is *one who does not leave the courtyard through the gate.* When you can finally take a step forward, make that step without hesitation. A moment's hesitation can lead to a lifetime of regret. Do not miss the opportunity.

Line 3
The third line is *one who does not follow the rules, and is filled with regret.* Ignoring your limits will have unpleasant consequences-and you will have only yourself to blame.

Line 4
The fourth line is *one who follows the rules and regulations.* Acceptance is key to a successful endeavor. If you can advance, by all means take the necessary steps forward. If you cannot, then retreat without complaint. In many cases, your limits will follow naturally from your circumstances.

Line 5
The fifth line is *one who willingly follows the rules and regulations.* If you think to place limitations on others, you must first place them on yourself. If you can withstand these limitations while staying content, then you can do as you wish. If you cannot, then you have no right to impose them on others.

Line 6
The sixth line is *one who unwillingly follows the rules and regulations.* The final goal will always be to find truth, but do not be harsh upon those who cannot find it-even yourself. Rather, practice gentleness and truth will present itself in due time.

61. Chung Fu - Inner Truth

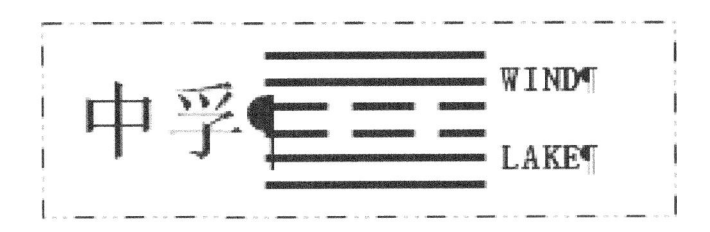

中孚 ☴ WIND
☱ LAKE

The representation

Judgment
Inner truth is the most of important of all virtues. Persevere in uncovering truth and remaining true to yourself and those who depend on you.

Image
Imagine the wind over the lake. This is the image of inner truth. Do not rush into hasty judgments. Rather, only act when everything is sure and correct-always seeking truth where it can be found.

Analysis

Inner truth is desirable in all situations. But when you face conflict and are convinced you are correct, do not pick a fight and push your ideals on others. While inner truth is important, it does no one good if you let your negative inclinations spur your actions. Approach life with a calm gentleness that will allow you to commune with the *Sage* and seek the truth. It will arrive in its own time. Do not force that truth on others, for this will also lead to demise. Rather, slowly introduce them to the power of the *Sage* and let *Him* do the rest.

Line-by-line reading

Line 1
The first line is *one who prepares himself while avoiding intrigues.* If you prepare yourself both inside and out, strength and success will

follow you-and it is best to walk this path alone.

Line 2
The second line is *a crane calling out to its offspring from their nest.* Others will know your mind by how you conduct yourself. Reflect upon yourself and identify where you can improve so that you will attract other people of good will.

Line 3
The third line is *one who finds his comrades.* Love others, but do not rely on them for your inner peace-that must come from you. Do not let the inclinations of others affect you too strongly.

Line 4
The fourth line is *one who is like a nearly-full moon, and whose horse has run away.* Make sure that your motivations remain grounded in the *Sage* and not in your ego. If you do the latter, you will meet failure.

Line 5
The fifth line is *one who is sincere and thus strengthens his unions.* If you constantly strive to improve yourself, you will meet with success and lead others thereto. The *Sage* will guide you.

Line 6
The sixth line is *one who tries to climb to the heavens.* Do not force others to accept truth. Rather, improve on yourself first and trust that others will follow suit.

62. Hsiao Kuo - Preponderance of the Small

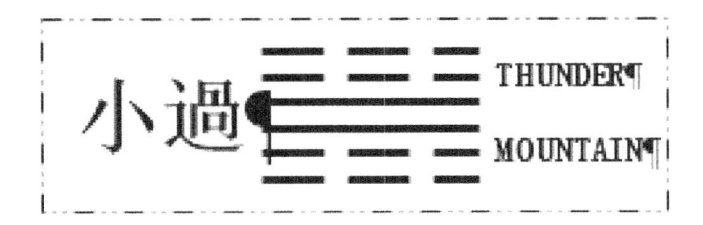

小過 ䷽ THUNDER
MOUNTAIN

The representation

Judgment
You will meet with good fortune only if you confine yourself to small actions that are within your capacity.

Image
Imagine the thunders booming above the mountains. It is a warning that you must scrupulously attend to your responsibilities in everything as appropriate to the circumstances.

Analysis

You are met with great trials, but you will succeed if you know that you must approach them with humility. Do not let anger, desire, or other negative inclinations fuel your actions. Rather, look to how you can change from within and become a better person. Ponder what you can do to remain steadfast in your principles and make small steps toward progress. Overreaching will lead to your downfall. Take things one small step at time, and let the bigger picture take care of itself.

Line-by-line reading

Line 1
The first line is *a bird who flies and meets with evil.* You are not ready to fly yet, so be patient and ask for the guidance of the *Sage*. If you fly prematurely, you will injure yourself.

Line 2
The second line is *one who passes by his ancestors.* Sometimes it may be appropriate to break the rules, so long as this is done from a sense of duty and with humility.

Line 3
The third line is *one who is unprepared in the face of evil and thus falls prey to injury.* If you succumb to your ego and become overconfident, you will meet with failure. Stay upright and just in your conduct, and the answers will come in due time.

Line 4
The fourth line is *one who passes by without meeting.* Let those who would influence you wrongly pass by like the breeze, taking and receiving nothing from you. Take no action, but turn to the *Higher Power* for guidance.

Line 5
The fifth line is *thick clouds that bring no rain.* If you are alone, you will fail. Look for others who will influence you correctly to avoid failure. They must be grounded in the *Sage,* as well.

Line 6
The sixth line is *one who passes another by but does not meet with him.* If you want to avoid failure, you must remain humble and principled. Do not give in to your appetites-they will be your downfall.

63. Chi Chi - After Completion

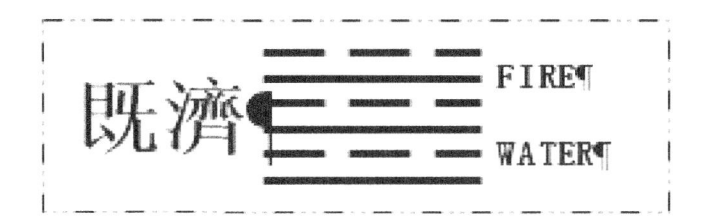

既濟 FIRE / WATER

The representation

Judgment
You will find success in small matters. If you remain persevering and listen to the *Higher Power*, you will meet with success. If you do not, the completion will not be as blessed.

Image
Imagine water over flames. This is the image of balanced conditions. If you want success, you will need to remain in the correct balance.

Analysis

Your life is no longer in chaos-and you must keep it that way. To remain in a peaceful state, you must remain vigilant, just as you must watch a boiling kettle to ensure that the water neither overflows nor evaporates. In the same way, you must make sure that no negative influences take root in your life and that you remain true to the principles that the *Sage* has taught you. Ready yourself for tribulation during this time of plenty so that you do not get caught off guard, whatever should happen next.

Line-by-line reading

Line 1
The first line is *one who slows his wheels and, like a fox, gets his tail wet.* While you are prosperous during this time, remember to

proceed slowly and with your principles close to your heart; in this way you will suffer only minor misfortune.

Line 2
The second line is *one who loses her carriage window screen but has no reason to look for it.* Do not seek the acceptance and approval of others. If you have it, then be happy. If you do not, do not force others to recognize you. Look within yourself and improve what you can.

Line 3
The third line is *one who conquers the Devil's Country, battling for three years.* Having struggled to gain your current success, do not throw it away by relying on inferior people. You will ultimately lose all that you have gained.

Line 4
The fourth line is *one who wears fine clothes that turn rags.* If you find yourself becoming too relaxed in this time of plenty, remember that there are many who can and will harm you. Be on guard, and do not become complacent in your tasks.

Line 5
The fifth line is *one who slaughters an ox but does not obtain true happiness.* If you do things for the wrong reasons, even if they are good, the *Sage* will not reward you and you will not meet with success.

Line 6
The sixth line is *one whose head is submerged in water.* Do not stop to think about what might have been. Rather, forge on and stay upright.

64. Wei Chi - Before Completion

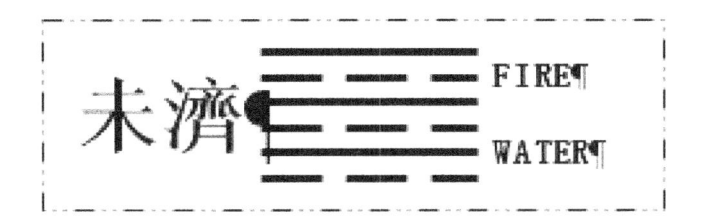

The representation

Judgment
All that you do before reaching the end will lead to your eventual success or failure. Do not let haste or inattentiveness keep you from finishing the journey.

Image
Imagine the fires sweeping over the waters. There is a proper conduct and attitude you must uphold to attain success. This is the condition and image of Before Completion.

Analysis

You are at a crossroads, and you need to make a choice. Like the transition from winter to spring, you are now going through a period of decision-making that forces you to make your life either better or worse. If you let your ego-desire, pride, anger-fuel your actions, then you will fall into the worst spring imaginable. If you act with the right motivations, then you will succeed. Remember, transition periods are vital because they dictate what will happen next. Do not make the mistake of embracing your negative inclinations for petty desires, only to suffer for them in the end.

Line-by-line reading

Line 1

The first line is *one who wets his tail, like a fox.* If you move too quickly, you will-ultimately-fail. Your public humiliation will lead to your demise.

Line 2
The second line is *one who slows his carriage wheels.* Do not let your ego guide you. It is now time to hang back and wait for an opportune moment. Wait patiently for the clear path to present itself.

Line 3
The third line is *one who attacks before completion, which brings misfortune.* During this transition period, you must remain grounded in your principles. It is not the time to strike, rather, it is time to reflect within yourself and prepare.

Line 4
The fourth line is *perseverance and disappearing remorse.* Persevere without doubts and without mercy, but always according to the good principles taught by the *Sage*. Continue on the correct path and you will get to your goal.

Line 5
The fifth line is *perseverance without remorse.* You have been and continue to be loyal to the *Sage* by upholding *His* principles and making them your own, and in this, you have become successful.

Line 6
The sixth line is *quiet feasting in confidence.* You are successful, but that does not give you leeway to become complacent. It is imperative that you remain alert and vigilant. Success does not success forever. Celebrate, but do not slacken your guard.

The Book of Divination and Wisdom

While the prophecies in the previous section of the book serve to nudge you in the right direction after you cast your hexagram, the readings can also serve as a more general source of wisdom and guidance. Apart from being a divination manual, the *I Ching* also serves as a book of wisdom and strength.

Even without a hexagram, you can read through the *I Ching* divination manual and turn to it for advice. Reading between the lines and learning about the different values and teachings it contains is another part of integrating the *I Ching* into your daily life. It is not easy to remain principled and just, but the *I Ching* reminds us that the world is bigger than ourselves.

It is imperative that we remain in the counsel of those who can do us good, and remove from our lives those who will bring us harm. Whatever your situation, the *I Ching* has sound advice to lead you to wherever you need to go.

It is difficult to follow the oracles of the *I Ching,* not only because they are spoken in riddles, but also because sometimes it presents truths that we ourselves are not yet willing to accept. It is occasionally hard and painful to behold, but heeding the *I Ching's* advice will always lead you onto a better path.

Lastly, the world is bigger than ourselves. It is bigger, wider, and we will never be able to completely understand it. Rather than focusing on yourself, try throwing yourself outward to the world and seeing what will happen. But remember that you must be grounded in your own principles and those that the *Sage* has taught you.

Turn to the *I Ching* for advice. It will lead you down the path you were *meant* to tread.